Gooseberry patch

From our Kitchen to Yours

Healthy, Happy,
Homemade Meals

Table of Contents

Dedication

For every cook who wants to create healthy, happy and homemade foods for their family and friends.

••••••••••••••••••••

Appreciation

Thanks to everyone who shared their delightful and delicious recipes with us!

••••••••••••••••••••

Gooseberry Patch
An imprint of Globe Pequot
246 Goose Lane • Guilford, CT 06437

www.gooseberrypatch.com
1•800•854•6673

Welcome

Dear Friends,

There is nothing more satisfying than knowing that the homemade recipes you prepare for your family and friends are good for them, and will bring smiles to their faces. **Healthy, Happy, Homemade Meals** offers 325 lightened-up recipes that bring the perfect ingredients to your table...healthy dishes, happy presentations and homemade goodness.

Inside you'll find yummy breakfast recipes like good-for-you Carroty Bran Muffins (page 54) and oh-so-filling Black Bean Breakfast Burritos (page 32). Need a healthy lunch in a jiffy? Try a homemade Garden-Fresh Pesto Pizza (page 70), classic Caprese Salad (page 77) or Key West Burgers (page 82) with slices of fresh mango. Everyone needs a little snack once in awhile! Make it a happy and healthy one by choosing an easy-grab Mini Ham & Swiss Fritatta (page 148) or Baja Shrimp Quesadillas (page 141). Simple soup and bread combinations are always a hit. Make it special by serving Madge's Beefy Chili (page 168) with a slice of Miss Sallie's Light Cornbread (page 173). They will love it! Make dinnertime extra special by serving Cilantro Chicken Skillet (page 237) in tortilla bowls you make yourself. And, finally, there is always room for a little bit of sweetness. Treat them with simple desserts like Snowy Glazed Apple Squares (page 266) or Strawberry-Yogurt Mousse (page 277).

We hope this cookbook will bring satisfying new recipes to your cooking repertoire and that you will discover the joy of making homemade, healthy food from your own happy kitchen. Enjoy!

Sincerely,
Jo Ann & Vickie

Introduction

Make it Healthy

There is a lot of advice everywhere on eating "healthy" and understandably the word "healthy" can mean different things to different people. Eating healthier doesn't have to be complicated if you follow some common-sense suggestions, knowing you can still enjoy every bite. Of course, if you have a health concern such as severe allergies, heart disease or diabetes, then eating healthy has a specific meaning to you. Eating healthy should be a way of life that makes you feel better and still enjoy the food you love. Here are some tips on eating healthier every day.

1 **Fresh, Fresh, Fresh.** Eating fresh vegetables and fruits is always a goal when eating healthier. Fresh from your garden, the local farmers' market or from the produce section of your favorite grocery store, choose ingredients that look fresh and colorful. Then enjoy them as soon as you can.

2 **Keep food simple.** Who needs to add heavy sauces and gravies when a grilled piece of meat or roasted fresh veggies tastes so great?

3 **Read the label.** When you read the label on a purchased food product, the ingredients are listed in the order of their relative volume in the food, highest to lowest. The first 3 ingredients make up the bulk of the food. Unprocessed or minimally processed foods are always best. Processed foods often contain preservatives, salt and sugar. Choose foods like eggs, lean meats, fresh fruits and veggies, and whole-grain breads over processed foods with added ingredients you don't need.

4 **Choose the right fats.** Use heart-healthy fats such as canola and olive oil whenever you can. Fats are good for you...just choose the right ones. And be a bit creative such as using avocado on your toast instead of butter.

5 **Don't forget to snack.** Having a healthy snack between meals can help you not to overeat when mealtime comes around.

6 **Treat yourself and enjoy.** There is always room for a treat. Dark chocolate contains antioxidants and is relatively low in sugar. The oatmeal in your favorite oatmeal cookie may lower your cholesterol.

7 **Watch the calories, sodium (salt), sugar and saturated fat.** The USDA says that most adults need about 2000 calories a day. Keeping sodium under 2400mg a day is best. Avoid eating added sugar...choose natural sugars from fruits instead. Fat is a bit tricky, because there are good and bad fats. Try to limit saturated fat. Make it a goal to aim for less than 10 percent of your daily calories.

8 **Enjoy protein and fiber.** A good rule for eating protein is to aim for eating one third of your body weight in grams, such as 50g per day if you're 150 pounds. High-fiber foods are good for you for lots of reasons, but importantly, they take longer for your body to digest so they make you feel less hungry. Try to eat at least 3g per serving.

Make it Happy

One of the greatest pleasures of life is sitting around the table with family & friends to enjoy a good meal. And when you present the dish you have made in a special way, and in an environment that is pleasant and calming, the food will taste better and the family will look forward to coming to the table to share the food and time together. Here are some tips for making mealtime a happy one.

1 Presentation of a food or recipe simply means how you give it to the person that is going to eat it. Think about how fun it is to sit at a restaurant and have the server present a beautiful plate of food to you, thoughtfully arranged on the plate. Presenting the food

doesn't have to be difficult or time-consuming. Choose plates in colors that work well with the colors of the food. White dishes are always a good choice. Garnish with a simple slice of lemon or a sprig of parsley or dill.

2 Turn off the devices and have some fun table talk. Take time to eat...don't hurry and eat just to fill your stomach. Enjoy every bite and visit about the day.

Make it Homemade

Making a meal at home and sharing it together has so many benefits. Make the process of creating the meal entertaining and joyful. Here are some good reasons for making your meal right in your own kitchen.

1 Preparing a meal together is a great family experience for any age. Even the little ones can help stir and add ingredients and feel a part of the meal prep that is so much fun.

2 Eating at home ensures you know where the ingredients come from and that they are fresh and good. You make the choice of what ingredients go into each dish and make the decisions about the food you are eating.

3 You'll be surprised how much money you will save by preparing food at home. Plan ahead when you are shopping so you can choose ingredients that can be used in several dishes.

RECIPE NOTES & NUTRITION FACTS

The recipes in this book were chosen or developed to be lighter and healthier than some of the recipes you may have used in the past. This means they may contain fewer calories, less fat, less salt, less sugar or more fiber. At the bottom of each recipe, you will see that each recipe has been analyzed to determine the nutritional content of the recipe. To help you understand what the values mean, we recommend that you compare them to the FDA's recommended values.

Following are the FDA's Daily Recommendations for an adult eating a 2000 calorie per day diet. You can refer to these numbers as you are looking at the nutritional values of the recipes in this book. Of course, if you are a larger or active person, you probably have higher nutritional needs, and if you are a smaller or sedentary person, you probably have lower nutritional needs. In addition, children, and pregnant and lactating women have unique nutritional needs.

FDA DAILY RECOMMENDATIONS FOR THE AVERAGE AMERICAN ADULT:

Total Calories:	2000 calories
Total Fat:	65g
Saturated Fat:	20g
Cholesterol:	300mg
Sodium:	2400mg
Carbohydrates:	300g
Fiber:	25g
Protein:	50g

Nutritional Information Credits:
Elizabeth Dahlstrom Burnley, MS Nutritional Sciences
Mary Kuster-Shell, BS Food Science
Crystal Tallman, MFCS Dietetics, RD, CSO, LD

CALCULATING THE NUTRITIONAL ANALYSIS

Ingredients in a product can vary slightly according to brands and natural differences in the ingredients. The nutritional analyses were based on typical brands and ingredients of products available at the time of printing.

With each recipe we have given a yield amount as well as a serving amount. The nutritional analysis is based on the serving amount. That is, the yield may be 24 cookies but it serves 12. That means that each person would be served 2 cookies.

Garnishes and optional ingredients were not included in the nutritional analysis.

Salt and pepper to taste: When the recipe indicates this, salt and pepper were not included in the nutritional analysis.

For frostings: When testing recipes, we based the nutritional analysis on what was actually used or shown in the photo.

For dressings: When the recipe calls for dressing, the entire dressing recipe was assumed to be used and all is included in the nutritional analysis.

For sauces: When testing the recipes, we based the nutritional analysis on the amount of sauce that was actually used per serving, not including extra leftover sauce.

Chapter One

Good-Start Breakfasts

Make it a **Great Beginning to Your Day** with healthy and happy choices made right in your own kitchen. If time is short, try a hearty bowl of Fruity Cinnamon Oatmeal topped with pomegranate seeds, or a Best-Ever Breakfast Bar. Time to sit and relax in the morning? Enjoy an unhurried breakfast with your family by baking a pan of Blackberry Buckle or a Ham & Tomato Pie. Just add a steamy pot of tea or fresh-brewed coffee and you are ready to start your day right!

Kristy Markners, *Fort Mill, SC*

Baked Breakfast Goodness

My two-year-old daughter just loves oatmeal. I got tired of fixing her the same old instant packet everyday, so I came up with this recipe. Sometimes we add some fresh fruit on top after it is baked. I like it just as much as she does!

Makes 4 servings

¼ c. unsweetened applesauce
¼ c. sugar
3 T. egg white substitute, beaten
½ c. 2% milk or unsweetened almond milk
1½ c. multi-grain hot cereal, uncooked
1 t. baking powder
½ t. cinnamon
⅛ t. ground ginger
1 banana, diced
¼ c. dried wild blueberries

Stir together applesauce, sugar, egg white and milk in a bowl. Add cereal, baking powder and spices; stir until well combined. Fold in fruit. Spoon into an 8"x6" baking pan sprayed with non-stick vegetable spray. Bake, uncovered, at 350 degrees for 30 minutes.

Nutrition Per Serving: 279 calories, 3g fat, 0g sat fat, 2mg cholesterol, 158mg sodium, 60g carbohydrate, 10g fiber, 26g sugars, 9g protein.

Judy Mitchell, *Huntley, IL*

Judy's Famous Banana Muffins

Our local newspaper featured me as "Cook of the Week" with this recipe! I found the original recipe many years ago and have revised it over the years. It's a favorite of family & friends.

Makes one dozen, serves 12

3 very ripe bananas, mashed
2 eggs, beaten
½ c. canola oil
½ c. plus 1 T. sugar, divided
½ c. quick-cooking oats, uncooked
½ c. whole-wheat flour
½ c. all-purpose flour
½ c. wheat germ
1 t. vanilla extract
1 t. baking powder
½ t. baking soda
¼ t. salt
¼ c. chopped walnuts

In a large bowl, stir together bananas, eggs, oil and ½ cup sugar until combined. Add remaining ingredients except walnuts and remaining sugar; stir just until blended. Spoon batter into 12 paper-lined muffin cups, filling about ⅔ full. Sprinkle tops with walnuts and remaining sugar. Bake at 350 degrees for 20 to 25 minutes, until golden and a toothpick tests clean. Let muffins cool in tin for 5 minutes; remove to a wire rack and cool completely.

Nutrition Per Serving: 238 calories, 12g fat, 1g sat fat, 31mg cholesterol, 155mg sodium, 29g carbohydrate, 3g fiber, 13g sugars, 5g protein.

Judy's Famous Banana Muffins

Asparagus & Mushroom Omelet

Audrey Lett, *Newark, DE*

Asparagus & Mushroom Omelet

A delicious way to savor the first tender asparagus of springtime. Add a sprinkle of shredded cheese, if you like.

Makes 3 servings

½ lb. asparagus, trimmed and cut into
   1-inch pieces
2 T. butter, divided
½ lb. sliced mushrooms
1 clove garlic, minced
4 eggs, lightly beaten
2 T. skim milk
¾ t. dried basil or thyme
½ t. salt
⅛ t. pepper

In a saucepan over medium heat, cover asparagus with water. Bring to a boil and cook until crisp-tender, about 4 minutes; drain. In a skillet over medium heat, melt one tablespoon butter. Sauté mushrooms and garlic in butter until tender and moisture has evaporated, 5 to 7 minutes. Add mushroom mixture to asparagus; keep warm. In a bowl, whisk together eggs, milk and seasonings. Melt remaining butter in skillet; swirl to coat bottom and sides. Add egg mixture. As eggs cook, gently lift up edges with a spatula and let uncooked egg run underneath until set. Spoon asparagus mixture onto one half of omelet. Slide omelet onto a plate; fold over. Cut into wedges.

Nutrition Per Serving: 202 calories, 14g fat, 7g sat fat, 269mg cholesterol, 508mg sodium, 8g carbohydrate, 3g fiber, 3g sugars, 12g protein.

Karen Jones, *Baltimore, MD*

Cinnamon Apple-Raisin Muffins

These are so easy to make and so healthy made with whole-wheat flour and applesauce.

Makes one dozen, serves 12

1 c. all-purpose flour
1 c. whole-wheat flour
¾ t. baking soda
½ t. salt
1 t. cinnamon
¾ c. unsweetened applesauce
¼ c. oil
½ c. sugar
2 eggs, beaten
1 t. vanilla extract
2 c. apples, peeled, cored and diced
1 c. raisins
½ c. chopped walnuts

In a bowl, stir together flours, baking soda, salt and cinnamon; set aside. In a separate large bowl, beat applesauce, oil and sugar with an electric mixer on low speed for 2 minutes. Add eggs and vanilla; beat for one minute and set aside. Add flour mixture to applesauce mixture; stir just until moist. Fold in remaining ingredients. Spoon batter into 12 paper-lined muffin cups, filling ⅔ full. Bake at 400 degrees for 25 to 30 minutes, until a toothpick inserted in center tests clean. Remove muffins from tin to a wire rack; serve warm or cooled.

Nutrition Per Serving: 247 calories, 9g fat, 1g sat fat, 31mg cholesterol, 193mg sodium, 39g carbohydrate, 3g fiber, 21g sugars, 5g protein.

Jill Ball, *Highland, UT*

Jill's Banana Butter

This is a great breakfast butter...I spread it on toast, English muffins and bagels. I even like to give a crock of this butter along with fresh bagels as a yummy birthday breakfast.

Makes 3 cups, serves 12

4 ripe bananas, sliced
3 T. lemon juice
1½ c. sugar
1 t. pumpkin pie spice

Place bananas and lemon juice in a food processor; pulse until smooth. Transfer mixture to a saucepan and stir in remaining ingredients. Bring to a boil over medium-high heat. Reduce heat and simmer 15 minutes; stir often. Spoon into an airtight container; cover and keep refrigerated.

Nutrition Per Serving: 133 calories, 0g fat, 0g sat fat, 0mg cholesterol, 1mg sodium, 34g carbohydrate, 1g fiber, 30g sugars, 0g protein.

Carol Lytle, *Columbus, OH*

Blackberry Buckle

We love to serve this coffee cake for special breakfasts or on the weekends.

Makes 9 servings

2 c. all-purpose flour
2½ t. baking powder
¼ t. salt
½ c. butter
¾ c. sugar
1 egg, beaten
½ c. milk
2 c. blackberries

Stir together flour, baking powder and salt; set aside. In a separate bowl, blend butter and sugar until light and fluffy. Add egg and beat well. Add flour mixture and milk alternately to egg mixture, beating until smooth. Pour into a greased 9"x9" baking pan; top with blackberries and Crumb Topping. Bake at 350 degrees for 50 to 60 minutes, until golden. Serve warm.

CRUMB TOPPING:
½ c. all-purpose flour
½ c. sugar
½ t. cinnamon
¼ c. butter

Sift together flour, sugar and cinnamon. Cut in butter until mixture resembles coarse crumbs.

Nutrition Per Serving: 373 calories, 14g total fat, 10g sat fat, 57mg cholesterol, 353mg sodium, 55g carbohydrate, 1g fiber, 31g sugars, 7g protein.

Blackberry Buckle

Holly Jackson, *St. George, UT*

Ham & Feta Cheese Omelet

The feta cheese in this omelet makes it so rich and yummy! We like to serve this with whole-grain toast and blackberry jam.

Makes one serving

2 eggs, beaten
¼ c. low-fat crumbled feta cheese
¼ c. cucumber, diced
1 T. green onion, chopped
¼ c. cooked ham, cubed
⅓ c. sliced black olives
salt and pepper to taste
Garnish: salsa

Combine all ingredients except salsa in a bowl; mix well. Pour into a lightly greased sauté pan or small skillet. Without stirring, cook over low heat until set. Fold over; transfer to serving plate. Serve with salsa.

Nutrition Per Serving: 339 calories, 19g total fat, 7g sat fat, 483mg cholesterol, 636mg sodium, 8g carbohydrate, 0g fiber, 2g sugars, 27g protein.

⁓ Healthy Fact ⁓

One egg has only 70 calories but has 7 grams of high-quality protein, along with iron, vitamins, minerals and carotenoids. There is a lot of good-for-you packed in that little shell!

Joshua Logan, *Corpus Christi, TX*

Egg & Bacon Quesadillas

I make these quesadillas on weekends when I have plenty of time to enjoy it. Serve with a cup of yogurt or some fresh fruit.

Serves 4

2 T. butter, divided
4 8-inch flour tortillas
5 eggs, beaten
½ c. skim milk
8-oz. pkg. low-fat shredded Cheddar cheese
2 slices bacon, crisply cooked and crumbled
Optional: salsa, plain yogurt

Lightly spread about ¼ teaspoon butter on one side of each tortilla; set aside. In a bowl, beat eggs and milk until combined. Pour egg mixture into a hot, lightly greased skillet; cook and stir over medium heat until done. Remove scrambled eggs to a dish and keep warm. Melt remaining butter in the skillet and add a tortilla, buttered-side down. Layer with ¼ of the cheese, ½ of the eggs and ½ of the bacon. Top with ¼ of the cheese and a tortilla, buttered-side up. Cook about one to 2 minutes on each side, until golden. Repeat with remaining ingredients. Cut each into 4 wedges and serve with salsa and plain yogurt, if desired.

Nutrition Per Serving: 476 calories, 27g fat, 14g sat fat, 286mg cholesterol, 926mg sodium, 27g carbohydrate, 1g fiber, 4g sugars, 30g protein.

Egg & Bacon Quesadillas

Crystal Shook, *Catawba, NC*

Peanutty Breakfast Wrap

In a hurry every morning? Don't leave home without a healthy breakfast!

Serves 2

8-inch whole-wheat tortilla
1 T. creamy peanut butter
1 T. non-fat vanilla yogurt
1 T. honey
¼ c. granola
¼ c. blueberries or diced strawberries

Spread one side of tortilla with peanut butter and yogurt. Drizzle with honey; sprinkle with granola and fruit. Roll up tightly; slice in half. Serve immediately, or wrap tightly in plastic wrap and refrigerate.

Nutrition Per Serving: 248 calories, 10g fat, 2g sat fat, 0mg cholesterol, 302mg sodium, 37g carbohydrate, 5g fiber, 15g sugars, 7g protein.

Hannah Hopkins, *Plainfield, VT*

Mother's Maple Spice Granola

I come from a family of six kids. This was one of my mother's yummy recipes that we took to school. I still love it!

Serves 8

¾ c. maple syrup
½ c. butter, melted
1 t. vanilla extract
1 t. cinnamon
1 t. nutmeg
2 c. long-cooking oats, uncooked
1½ c. unsweetened flaked coconut
⅓ c. sesame seed
1 c. raisins
½ c. chopped walnuts

Mix maple syrup and butter thoroughly in a large bowl; add vanilla and spices. Toss all the remaining ingredients together; stir into syrup mixture. Spoon into a greased 13"x9" baking pan. Bake at 350 degrees for 45 minutes, stirring every 15 minutes. Cool mixture before serving.

Nutrition Per Serving: 517 calories, 27g fat, 13g sat fat, 31mg cholesterol, 13mg sodium, 65g carbohydrate, 8g fiber, 32g sugars, 10g protein.

Happy Presentation

A simple brown paper bag makes a quick container for this yummy granola for a take-along breakfast. Add a good morning note on the outside of the bag just for fun.

Mother's Maple Spice Granola

Ham & Tomato Pie

Elizabeth Blackstone, *Racine, WI*

Ham & Tomato Pie

Summer's best flavors are blended in this quiche-style recipe...sweet fresh basil, juicy plum tomatoes and crisp green onions.

Serves 8

8-oz. pkg. cooked ham, diced
1/2 c. green onions, sliced
9-inch frozen pie crust, thawed
1 T. Dijon mustard
1 c. low-fat shredded mozzarella cheese, divided
2 plum tomatoes, thinly sliced
1 egg
1/3 c. 2% milk
1 T. fresh basil, chopped
1/8 t. pepper

Sauté ham and green onions in a large non-stick skillet over medium heat 5 minutes or until ham is brown and any liquid evaporates. Brush bottom of pie crust evenly with mustard; sprinkle with 1/2 cup mozzarella cheese. Spoon ham mixture evenly over cheese and top with sliced tomatoes arranged in a single layer. Beat egg and milk with a fork until blended; pour over tomatoes. Sprinkle evenly with basil, pepper and remaining cheese. Bake on lowest oven rack at 425 degrees for 20 to 23 minutes, until lightly golden and set. Cool on a wire rack 20 minutes. Cut into wedges to serve.

Nutrition Per Serving: 203 calories, 12g fat, 4g sat fat, 50mg cholesterol, 580mg sodium, 13g carbohydrate, 1g fiber, 1g sugars, 11g protein.

Kathy Grashoff, *Fort Wayne, IN*

Blueberry Buckle Coffee Cake

Fresh blueberries are a summertime treat to be savored and we love them. This coffee cake showcases them well!

Makes 9 servings

2 c. all-purpose flour
3/4 c. sugar
2 1/2 t. baking powder
3/4 t. salt
1/4 c. butter
3/4 c. 2% milk
2 c. blueberries

Mix together all ingredients except berries. Beat for 30 seconds; carefully fold in berries. Spread batter into a greased 9"x9" baking pan; sprinkle with Crumb Topping. Bake at 375 degrees for 45 to 50 minutes.

CRUMB TOPPING:

1/4 c. brown sugar, packed
1/3 c. all-purpose flour
3 T. butter, softened
1/2 t. cinnamon

Mix all ingredients together until crumbly.

Nutrition Per Serving: 314 calories, 10g fat, 6g sat fat, 25mg cholesterol, 346mg sodium, 53g carbohydrate, 2g fiber, 27g sugars, 4g protein.

Becky Drees, *Pittsfield, MA*

Trail Mix Bagels

Perfect for an on-the-go breakfast or hike...a tasty energy boost!

Makes 4 servings

8-oz. pkg. low-fat cream cheese, softened
1 T. lemon juice
1/2 c. raisins
1 carrot, peeled and grated
1/3 c. trail mix, coarsely chopped, or
    sunflower kernels
4 whole-grain or sesame bagels, split

Place cream cheese in a bowl. Add remaining ingredients except bagels; stir until well blended and creamy. Spread between sliced bagels.

Nutrition Per Serving: 480 calories, 14g fat, 6g sat fat, 31mg cholesterol, 714mg sodium, 74g carbohydrate, 5g fiber, 21g sugars, 17g protein.

Evelyn Bennett, *Salt Lake City, UT*

Easy Eggs Benedict

We love to serve this elegant breakfast when we have company...everyone is always so impressed!

Serves 8

8 eggs
3/4 c. light mayonnaise
1/4 c. whipping cream, whipped
1 t. lemon zest
1 T. lemon juice
4 English muffins, split and toasted
4 slices Canadian bacon, halved

Lightly grease a large skillet; add water to a depth of 2 inches. Bring to a boil; reduce heat, maintaining a light simmer. Working in batches to poach 4 eggs at a time, break eggs, one at a time, into a cup; slip egg into water, holding cup close to water. Simmer 5 minutes or until done. Remove eggs with a slotted spoon; trim edges of eggs, if desired. Set aside. Combine mayonnaise and salt in a small saucepan. Cook over low heat, stirring constantly, 3 minutes. Stir in whipped cream, lemon zest and lemon juice; remove from heat and keep warm. Arrange bacon on muffin halves; top each bacon piece with a poached egg. Spoon reserved sauce over eggs.

Nutrition Per Serving: 229 calories, 13g fat, 4g sat fat, 203mg cholesterol, 623mg sodium, 16g carbohydrate, 1g fiber, 2g sugars, 11g protein.

Easy Eggs Benedict

Eleanor Dionne, *Beverly, MA*

Sweet Potato Pancakes

We enjoy these healthy pancakes for a special breakfast...they're just a little different from the traditional potato pancake.

Makes 4 servings, 2 pancakes each

1 c. sweet potato, peeled and grated
1 c. white potato, peeled and grated
1 t. salt, divided
1 c. carrots, peeled and grated
2 T. onion, grated
4 eggs, beaten
1/3 c. all-purpose flour
1/4 c. fresh parsley, chopped
juice of 1/2 lemon
pepper to taste
1/8 t. nutmeg
3 T. plain non-fat Greek yogurt
1 T. fresh chives, snipped

Place potatoes in a colander over a bowl. Sprinkle with 1/2 teaspoon salt; let stand for 15 minutes. Rinse well; squeeze out well to remove all the excess water. In a large bowl, combine potatoes with carrots, onion, eggs, flour, parsley, lemon juice, seasonings and remaining salt. Mix well and form into 8 pancakes. Cook on a lightly greased griddle over medium-high heat until crisp and golden on both sides. Serve pancakes topped with a dollop of yogurt and a sprinkle of chives.

Nutrition Per Serving: 148 calories, 3g fat, 1g sat fat, 94mg cholesterol, 673mg sodium, 24g carbohydrate, 3g fiber, 4g sugars, 7g protein.

Jill Ball, *Highland, UT*

Fruity Cinnamon Oatmeal

There's nothing more perfect than sitting by the fireplace watching the snow fall while eating a warm bowl of oatmeal. This recipe is one of our favorites...it's warm, filling and yummy.

Makes 4 servings

3 c. water
4-inch cinnamon stick
1 1/2 c. long-cooking oats, uncooked
1 apple, peeled, cored, and diced
3 T. maple syrup, divided
1 t. cinnamon
1/2 t. allspice
Garnish: pomegranate seeds, cinnamon

Combine water and cinnamon stick in a small saucepan. Bring to a boil over high heat. Stir in oats and apple; reduce heat to medium. Cook for 5 to 10 minutes, stirring often, to desired consistency. Remove from heat; discard cinnamon stick. Stir in 2 tablespoons syrup and spices. Ladle into bowls; top each with a drizzle of remaining syrup, some pomegranate seeds and a sprinkle of cinnamon.

Nutrition Per Serving: 180 calories, 2g fat, 0g sat fat, 0mg cholesterol, 2mg sodium, 38g carbohydrate, 4g fiber, 15g sugars, 4g protein.

Fruity Cinnamon Oatmeal

Triann Benson, *Plano, TX*

Benson's Ultimate Pancakes

The entire family will ask for more of these amazing pancakes!

Makes about one dozen, serves 6

1½ c. all-purpose flour
1 T. baking powder
1 T. sugar
1 t. salt
1¼ c. skim milk
1 egg yolk, beaten
2 T. butter, melted
1 T. vanilla extract
2 egg whites
1½ c. blueberries
Garnish: maple syrup, low-fat whipped
   topping and/or blueberries

Combine first 8 ingredients in a large bowl. Beat egg whites with an electric mixer at high speed until stiff peaks form. Gently fold into batter. Pour batter by ⅓ cupfuls onto a greased hot griddle. Spoon several blueberries on top of just-poured batter. Cook until bubbles appear on the surface; flip and continue cooking for 2 to 3 more minutes, until golden. Garnish as desired.

Nutrition Per Serving: 215 calories, 5g fat, 3g sat fat, 42mg cholesterol, 683mg sodium, 35g carbohydrate, 2g fiber, 5g sugars, 7g protein.

Joyce LaMure, *Sequim, WA*

Cranberry-Orange Scones

I received this recipe from a friend a few years ago. They're not only yummy, but quick & easy to make.

Serves 10

2 c. biscuit baking mix
½ c. sugar
½ c. butter, softened
1 egg, beaten
½ c. dried cranberries
½ c. chopped pecans
1 T. orange zest
2½ to 3 T. buttermilk
Garnish: beaten egg white, sanding sugar

Combine baking mix, sugar and butter until crumbly. Make a well in the center and add egg; stir to blend. Stir in cranberries, pecans and zest. Add buttermilk as needed for dough to form a soft ball. Place dough on lightly floured surface and knead 3 or 4 times. Flatten dough and shape into an 8-inch circle. Using a serrated knife, cut dough in triangles. Brush with egg white and garnish with sugar. Arrange on a lightly oiled baking sheet and bake at 400 degrees for 10 to 15 minutes, or until golden.

Nutrition Per Serving: 295 calories, 18g fat, 7g sat fat, 44mg cholesterol, 343mg sodium, 32g carbohydrate, 1g fiber, 17g sugars, 3g protein.

Cranberry-Orange Scones

Breakfast Salad with Poached Eggs

Kelly Gray, *Weston, WV*

Breakfast Salad with Poached Eggs

This dish may sound odd, but it is really delicious...quick to make too. I serve it often for brunch, while my son requests it often for dinner. I like to add two poached eggs per salad, but you may prefer just one.

Makes 4 servings

4 slices bacon, halved
2 c. water
2 t. vinegar
8 eggs, divided
8 c. spring lettuce mix
1 c. low-fat shredded Cheddar cheese
1 c. sliced mushrooms
1 c. sliced black olives
4 roma tomatoes, quartered

Cook bacon in a skillet over medium heat until crisp; drain. Set aside. In a skillet over medium-high heat, bring water and vinegar to a simmer. Crack 2 eggs into water. Cook for 5 to 7 minutes, to desired doneness. Remove eggs with a slotted spoon; repeat with remaining eggs. Divide lettuce among 4 plates. With a slotted spoon, place 2 eggs atop lettuce on each plate; sprinkle with cheese while still hot Arrange vegetables around eggs; arrange bacon on top. Serve immediately.

Nutrition Per Serving: 416 calories, 30g fat, 10g sat fat, 417mg cholesterol, 920mg sodium, 12g carbohydrate, 3g fiber, 3g sugars, 27g protein.

Amy Bradsher, *Roxboro, NC*

Banana Bread Pancakes

The first time I made these unusual-looking pancakes, my Little Man didn't want to try them, but he was hooked at the first nibble. My Big Helper, on the other hand, took one bite and yelled, "Mommy! I'll give you a hundred hugs and kisses for these!"

Makes about one dozen pancakes, serves 6

2 c. whole-wheat flour
2 t. baking powder
1/4 t. salt
1 t. cinnamon
3/4 c. skim milk
4 T. honey
2 T. butter, melted
1 t. vanilla extract
3 ripe bananas, mashed
Garnish: maple syrup
Optional: chopped walnuts

In a large bowl, mix together flour, baking powder, salt and cinnamon. In a separate bowl, stir together milk, honey, butter and vanilla. Slowly pour milk mixture into flour mixture; stir well. Add bananas; stir to combine. Spoon batter by 1/3 cupfuls onto a lightly greased griddle over medium heat. Cook for 2 to 3 minutes, until bubbles begin to form on top; turn. Cook on other side for another 2 to 3 minutes, until golden. Serve topped with maple syrup and garnished with walnuts, if desired.

Nutrition Per Serving: 138 calories, 2g fat, 1g sat fat, 5mg cholesterol, 138mg sodium, 28g carbohydrate, 3g fiber, 11g sugars, 4g protein.

Herbed Sausage Quiche

Cherylann Smith, *Efland, NC*

Herbed Sausage Quiche

Serve this quiche right from the table...it is so pretty!

Makes 8 servings

9-inch frozen pie crust, thawed
1 c. ground pork breakfast sausage, browned
   and drained
3 eggs, beaten
1 c. 2% milk
1 c. low-fat shredded Cheddar cheese
1 sprig fresh rosemary, chopped
1½ t. Italian seasoning
¼ t. salt
¼ t. pepper

Bake pie crust according to package directions. Mix together remaining ingredients in a bowl; spread into baked crust. Bake, uncovered, at 450 degrees for 15 minutes. Reduce oven temperature to 350 degrees, cover with foil and bake 9 more minutes. Cut into wedges to serve.

Nutrition Per Serving: 248 calories, 17g fat, 5g sat fat, 87mg cholesterol, 485mg sodium, 13g carbohydrate, 0g fiber, 2g sugars, 11g protein.

Kitchen Helper

Baking the pie crust before you add all of the ingredients keeps the bottom of the quiche from becoming soggy. You can also brush egg whites over the bottom of the crust before adding the liquid ingredients to ward off sogginess.

Carla Turner, *Salem, OR*

Make-Ahead French Toast

This wonderful make-ahead dish is perfect for brunches. With the prep time being the day before, I'm free to visit with friends & family.

Serves 15

3 T. butter
2 baking apples, peeled, cored and sliced
⅓ c. brown sugar, packed
1 T. dark corn syrup
1 t. cinnamon
8 1-inch thick slices French bread
3 eggs, beaten
1 c. milk
1 t. vanilla extract

Melt butter in a heavy skillet over medium heat. Reduce heat to medium-low; add apples and cook, stirring occasionally, until tender. Stir in brown sugar, corn syrup and cinnamon. Cook and stir until brown sugar dissolves. Pour apple mixture into two lightly greased 9" pie plates or one, 13"x9" baking pan. Arrange bread slices in one layer on top of apple mixture; set aside. In a medium bowl, whisk together remaining ingredients; pour over bread slices. Cover with plastic wrap and refrigerate overnight. Remove plastic wrap and bake at 375 degrees for 30 to 35 minutes, or until firm and golden. Cool 5 minutes in pan, then invert onto a serving platter.

Nutrition Per Serving: 202 calories, 4g fat, 2g sat fat, 44mg cholesterol, 356mg sodium, 33g carbohydrate, 2g fiber, 5g sugars, 8g protein.

Jackie Smulski, *Lyons, IL*

Scrambled Eggs & Lox

These eggs are sure to please everyone. We love them with toasted English muffins.

Serves 6

6 eggs, beaten
1 T. fresh dill, minced
1 T. fresh chives, minced
1 T. green onion, minced
pepper to taste
2 T. butter
4-oz. pkg. smoked salmon, diced

Whisk together eggs, herbs, onion and pepper. Melt butter in a large skillet over medium heat. Add egg mixture and stir gently with a fork or spatula until eggs begin to set. Stir in salmon and continue cooking eggs to desired doneness.

Nutrition Per Serving: 128 calories, 9g fat, 4g sat fat, 201mg cholesterol, 450mg sodium, 0g carbohydrate, 0g fiber, 0g sugars, 10g protein.

Meg Dickinson, *Champaign, IL*

Black Bean Breakfast Burritos

My husband and I love the idea of eating breakfast for dinner so I tried this combination, and it was a huge hit.

Makes 6 burritos, serves 6

2 T. olive oil
½ c. onion, chopped
½ c. green pepper, chopped
3 cloves garlic, minced
16-oz. can low-sodium black beans, drained and rinsed
10-oz. diced tomatoes with green chiles
1 t. fajita seasoning mix
6 eggs
½ c. green onion, chopped
1 T. Fiesta Dip Mix
6 8-inch flour tortillas, warmed
½ c. low-fat shredded Cheddar cheese

Heat oil in a Dutch oven over medium heat. Add onion, green pepper and garlic; sauté until tender. Stir in beans, tomatoes and fajita seasoning. Bring to a simmer and let cook about 10 minutes. Meanwhile, in a bowl, whisk together eggs, green onion and one tablespoon Fiesta Dip Mix. Scramble egg mixture in a lightly greased skillet. To serve, top each tortilla with a spoonful of bean mixture, a spoonful of scrambled eggs and a sprinkle of cheese; roll up tortilla.

FIESTA DIP MIX:

2 T. dried parsley
4 t. dried, minced onion
4 t. chili powder
1 T. dried cumin
1 T. dried chives
1 t. salt

Mix all ingredients well; store in a small jar. Makes about ½ cup.

Nutrition Per Serving: 369 calories, 14g fat, 4g sat fat, 191mg cholesterol, 779mg sodium, 42g carbohydrate, 7g fiber, 6g sugars, 18g protein.

Black Bean Breakfast Burritos

California Omelet

Christina Mendoza, *Alamogordo, NM*

California Omelet

We love breakfast made with fresh ingredients...this omelet is perfect!

Serves 2

1 T. oil
3 eggs
¼ c. skim milk
salt and pepper to taste
1 avocado, pitted, peeled and sliced
2 green onions, diced
½ c. low-fat shredded Monterey Jack cheese

Heat oil in a skillet over medium-low heat. Whisk together eggs, milk, salt and pepper in a bowl; pour into skillet. Cook until eggs are lightly golden on bottom and partially set on top. Sprinkle with remaining ingredients; carefully fold omelet in half so toppings are covered. Reduce heat to medium-low and cook, uncovered, about 10 minutes.

Nutrition Per Serving: 363 calories, 30g fat, 7g sat fat, 290mg cholesterol, 247mg sodium, 10g carbohydrate, 6g fiber, 2g sugars, 16g protein.

Yvette Nelson, *British Columbia, Canada*

Fiesta Breakfast Strata

This is a recipe I created because I love Mexican food.

Serves 10

1 lb. lean ground beef
8-oz. can tomato sauce
2 t. chili powder
½ t. garlic powder
salt and pepper to taste
5 10-inch flour tortillas
16-oz. can refried beans, divided
8-oz. pkg. low-fat shredded sharp Cheddar cheese, divided
1 red pepper, diced
2 tomatoes, diced
5 green onions, chopped
salt and pepper to taste
Garnish: salsa

Brown ground beef in a skillet; drain. Add tomato sauce and seasonings. Simmer until mixture thickens; set aside. Line the bottom of a 9" springform pan with aluminum foil. Place a tortilla in the bottom of the pan. Spread half the refried beans on tortilla and top with half the ground beef mixture. Top with ⅓ of the cheese. Layer a second tortilla over cheese; sprinkle with half each red pepper, tomatoes and onions. Add a third tortilla and spread with remaining refried beans, beef mixture and ⅓ cheese. Layer on a fourth tortilla and top with remaining red pepper and tomatoes. Add last tortilla and cover with remaining cheese and onions. Bake, uncovered, at 350 degrees for one hour, or until heated through. Garnish with salsa.

Nutrition Per Serving: 303 calories, 11g fat, 5g sat fat, 41mg cholesterol, 802mg sodium, 30g carbohydrate, 4g fiber, 4g sugars, 21g protein.

Nancy Porter, *Fort Wayne, IN*

Berry-Picker's Reward Muffins

This recipe works well with blueberries and strawberries too.

Makes 20, serves 20

1/2 c. butter, softened
1 c. sugar
2 eggs, beaten
8-oz. container non-fat plain yogurt
1 t. vanilla extract
2 c. all-purpose flour
1 t. baking powder
1/2 t. baking soda
1/4 t. salt
1 c. raspberries

With an electric mixer on medium-high speed, beat softened butter for 30 seconds. Add sugar; beat until combined. Blend in eggs, yogurt and vanilla. Use a spoon to stir in dry ingredients until just moistened; fold in berries. Spoon batter into paper-lined or greased muffin cups, filling 2/3 full. Sprinkle with Topping. Bake at 400 degrees for 18 to 20 minutes, or until a toothpick tests clean. Cool in pan for 5 minutes; transfer to a wire rack to finish cooling.

TOPPING:

2 T. sugar
1/4 t. cinnamon
1/4 t. nutmeg

Combine all ingredients in a small bowl.

Nutrition Per Serving: 145 calories, 5g fat, 3g sat fat, 31mg cholesterol, 100mg sodium, 22g carbohydrate, 1g fiber, 12g sugars, 3g protein.

Susan Pribble-Moore, *Roanoke, VA*

Low-Fat Chocolate Oat Muffins

The grated zucchini in these muffins makes them so moist and yummy!

Makes one dozen, serves 12

2 c. oat flour
1/3 c. brown sugar, packed
1/3 c. baking cocoa
2 t. baking powder
1/2 t. baking soda
1/2 t. salt
1 c. dark chocolate chips
2/3 c. zucchini, finely grated
1 c. skim milk
1/3 c. honey
2 egg whites, beaten
Garnish: oatmeal

In a bowl, combine flour, brown sugar, baking cocoa, baking powder, baking soda and salt. Mix well; gently stir in chocolate chips. In a separate large bowl, combine remaining ingredients, except garnish; mix well. Add flour mixture to zucchini mixture; stir only until well combined. Spoon batter into muffin cups sprayed with non-stick vegetable spray, filling cups 2/3 full. Sprinkle oatmeal on top of muffins. Bake at 400 degrees for 18 to 20 minutes, until a toothpick tests clean. Cool muffin tin on a wire rack for 10 minutes; remove muffins from tin.

Nutrition Per Serving: 229 calories, 8g fat, 4g sat fat, 0mg cholesterol, 253mg sodium, 38g carbohydrate, 3g fiber, 26g sugars, 5g protein.

Low-Fat Chocolate Oat Muffins

Larissa Miller, *Bradley Beach, NJ*

Orange Yogurt Pancakes

These pancakes are easy to make, fluffy and delicious. My cousin shared a version of this recipe with me, and I've modified it a bit. Have some fun...add chopped fruit or nuts to the batter too.

Serves 4

1½ c. whole-wheat flour
1 T. brown sugar, packed
¾ t. baking powder
1½ t. baking soda
¼ t. salt
2 eggs
1½ c. non-fat vanilla yogurt
½ c. milk
½ c. orange juice
zest of 1 orange

In a large bowl, combine flour, brown sugar, baking powder, baking soda and salt; set aside. In a separate bowl, whisk eggs; stir in remaining ingredients. Add egg mixture to flour mixture. Stir until combined; let stand for several minutes. Pour batter by ¼ cupfuls onto an oiled griddle over medium-high heat. Cook until small bubbles form around the edges; flip and cook until other side is golden.

Nutrition Per Serving: 144 calories, 2g fat, 0g sat fat, 48mg cholesterol, 407mg sodium, 27g carbohydrate, 2g fiber, 9g sugars, 7g protein.

Mary Ann Lewis, *Olive Branch, MS*

Best-Ever Breakfast Bars

These chewy, nutty, healthy bars are great to grab in the morning for a perfect take-along breakfast.

Makes one dozen, serves 12

1 c. oat-based granola
1 c. quick-cooking oats, uncooked
½ c. all-purpose flour
¼ c. brown sugar, packed
⅛ t. cinnamon
½ c. unsalted mixed nuts, coarsely chopped
½ c. dried fruit, chopped into small pieces
2 T. ground flaxseed meal
¼ c. canola oil
⅓ c. honey
½ t. vanilla extract
1 egg, beaten

Combine granola and next 7 ingredients in a large bowl. Whisk together oil, honey and vanilla; stir into granola mixture. Add egg; stir to blend. Press mixture into a parchment paper-lined 8"x8" baking pan. Bake at 325 degrees for 30 to 35 minutes, until lightly golden around the edges. Remove from oven and cool 30 minutes to one hour. Slice into bars.

Nutrition Per Serving: 240 calories, 11g fat, 2g sat fat, 16mg cholesterol, 11mg sodium, 32g carbohydrate, 3g fiber, 13g sugars, 5g protein.

Best-Ever Breakfast Bars

Irene Whatling, *West Des Moines, IA*

Colorful Fruit Soup

This soup is so refreshing! My daughter requests it every summer. Freshly ground black pepper complements the sweet fruit wonderfully. Try it!

Makes 6 servings

1 c. seedless grapes, halved
1 c. blueberries
½ c. strawberries, hulled and diced
½ c. pineapple, peeled and diced
½ c. kiwi, peeled and diced
1 c. unsweetened apple juice
½ c. orange juice
¼ t. pepper

Combine fruit in a large bowl. In a measuring cup, mix juices and pepper; pour over fruit mixture. Stir gently. Cover and refrigerate until serving time.

Nutrition Per Serving: 73 calories, 0g fat, 0g sat fat, 0mg cholesterol, 3mg sodium, 18g carbohydrate, 2g fiber, 12g sugars, 1g protein.

Eleanor Dionne, *Beverly, MA*

Blueberry Cornmeal Pancakes

Since we like cornmeal muffins as well as anything with blueberries, it's no surprise that these pancakes became a family favorite.

Makes about 24 pancakes, serves 6

1 c. all-purpose flour
1 c. cornmeal
2 T. baking powder
1 T. sugar
1½ c. orange juice
3 T. canola oil
1 egg, beaten
1 c. blueberries, thawed if frozen
Garnish: fresh blueberries, light maple syrup

In a bowl, mix together flour, cornmeal, baking powder and sugar. Add juice, oil and egg; stir well. Gently fold in blueberries. Heat a lightly greased griddle over medium-high heat. Pour batter onto griddle, making small pancakes. Cook pancakes until bubbles appear around the edges; flip and cook on other side. Garnish as desired.

Nutrition Per Serving: 287 calories, 8g fat, 1g sat fat, 31mg cholesterol, 505mg sodium, 48g carbohydrate, 2g fiber, 9g sugars, 5g protein.

Blueberry Cornmeal Pancakes

Jenny Sisson, *Broomfield, CO*

Cranberry Buttermilk Scones

These tasty scones are one of our family favorites. The buttermilk makes them so tender and the cranberries add just the right amount of flavor and texture.

Serves 10

2 c. all-purpose flour
1/3 c. sugar
1/4 t. salt
1 1/2 t. baking powder
1/2 t. baking soda
6 T. butter
2/3 c. sweetened dried cranberries
1/2 c. buttermilk
1 egg
1 1/2 t. vanilla extract

Stir together first 5 ingredients; cut in butter with a pastry blender. Stir in cranberries.

Combine buttermilk, egg and vanilla; mix into flour mixture until just moistened. Drop dough in 10 tablespoonfuls onto a greased baking sheet. Bake at 375 degrees for 15 minutes or until set and golden.

Nutrition Per Serving: 219 calories, 8g fat, 5g sat fat, 37mg cholesterol, 215mg sodium, 34g carbohydrate, 1g fiber, 13g sugars, 4g protein.

Amy Butcher, *Columbus, GA*

Fluffy Baked Eggs

Who would have thought to combine pineapple and eggs? After you taste this yummy recipe, you'll see why!

Makes 12 servings

14 eggs, beaten
3 slices bacon, crisply cooked and crumbled
1 1/3 c. low-fat cottage cheese
8-oz. can crushed pineapple in own juice, drained
1 t. vanilla extract
Garnish: cooked bacon crumbles, chopped fresh parsley

In a bowl blend together eggs, bacon, cottage cheese, pineapple and vanilla; spoon into a greased 13"x9" baking pan. Bake, uncovered, at 350 degrees for 40 to 45 minutes, until center is set and a toothpick inserted in center comes out clean. Allow baking pan to stand 5 minutes before slicing. Garnish with cooked bacon crumbles and parsley; cut into squares.

Nutrition Per Serving: 163 calories, 10g fat, 3g sat fat, 227mg cholesterol, 261mg sodium, 4g carbohydrate, 1g fiber, 4g sugars, 13g protein.

Jill Burton, *Gooseberry Patch*

Baked Eggs in Tomatoes

So pretty for a brunch...a delicious way to enjoy tomatoes from the farmers' market. I like to use fresh corn, but frozen works just fine as well.

Makes 6 servings

6 tomatoes, tops cut off
1/4 t. pepper
1/2 c. corn, thawed if frozen
1/2 c. red pepper, diced
1/2 c. mushrooms, diced
2 T. cream cheese, softened and divided
6 eggs
2 t. fresh chives, minced
1/4 c. grated Parmesan cheese

With a spoon, carefully scoop out each tomato, creating shells. Sprinkle pepper inside tomatoes. Divide corn, red pepper and mushrooms among tomatoes; top each with one teaspoon cream cheese. In a bowl, whisk together eggs and chives. Divide egg mixture among tomatoes; top with Parmesan cheese. Place filled tomatoes in a lightly greased 2-quart casserole dish. Bake, uncovered, at 350 degrees until egg mixture is set, about 45 to 50 minutes. Serve warm.

Nutrition Per Serving: 143 calories, 8g fat, 3g sat fat, 194mg cholesterol, 167mg sodium, 9g carbohydrate, 2g fiber, 5g sugars, 10g protein.

Michelle Case, *Yardley, PA*

Breakfast Berry Parfait

We like all kinds of berries, so we make this combining all of our favorites!

Serves 2

1 c. bran & raisin cereal, divided
6-oz. container low-fat strawberry yogurt
1 c. strawberries, hulled and sliced
1/2 c. raspberries
1/4 c. blackberries

Layer half of the cereal and all of the yogurt in the 2 glasses. Add berries and top with remaining cereal.

Nutrition Per Serving: 192 calories, 2g fat, 1g sat fat, 3mg cholesterol, 214mg sodium, 44g carbohydrate, 7g fiber, 23g sugars, 6g protein.

Mom's Everything Waffles

Tamara Ahrens, *Sparta, MI*

Mom's Everything Waffles

The delicious flavors of peanut butter, pecans and blueberries come together in this one-of-a-kind breakfast favorite.

Makes 10 waffles, serves 10

1¼ c. all-purpose flour
1 T. baking powder
¼ t. salt
2 t. sugar
¾ c. plus 2 T. quick-cooking oats, uncooked
2 T. wheat germ
3 T. chopped pecans
2 eggs, beaten
2 T. reduced-fat peanut butter
½ c. plain Greek yogurt
2½ c. skim milk, divided
¾ c. fresh blueberries
Garnish: sugar-free maple syrup, fresh
   blueberries

Combine flour, baking powder, salt, sugar, oats, wheat germ and nuts in a large bowl; set aside. In a separate bowl, whisk together eggs, peanut butter, yogurt and 2 cups milk. Add to dry ingredients and stir. Add remaining milk as needed to get the consistency of applesauce. Fold in berries. Pour by ½ cupfuls onto a preheated waffle iron that has been sprayed with non-stick vegetable spray. Bake until crisp, according to manufacturer's directions. Serve with one tablespoon sugar-free maple syrup and blueberries.

Nutrition Per Serving: 199 calories, 5g fat, 1g sat fat, 43mg cholesterol, 141mg sodium, 30g carbohydrate, 2g fiber, 9g sugars, 9g protein.

Regina Ferrigno, *Delaware, OH*

Grammy's Overnight Pancakes

Whenever we visit Grammy, these yummy pancakes are on the breakfast table without fail. Usually they're surrounded by sausage or bacon, scrambled eggs and toast with jam.

Makes 2 dozen, serves 8

2 c. long-cooking oats, uncooked
2 c. plus ¼ c. buttermilk, divided
½ c. all-purpose flour
½ c. whole-wheat flour
2 t. sugar
1½ t. baking powder
1½ t. baking soda
¼ t. salt
2 eggs, beaten
2 T. butter, melted and cooled
oil for frying
Garnish: butter, warm maple syrup

Combine oats and 2 cups buttermilk in a bowl; cover and refrigerate overnight. To prepare pancakes, sift together flours, sugar, baking powder, baking soda and salt. Set aside. In a large bowl, beat together eggs and butter. Stir into oat mixture. Add flour mixture, stirring well. If batter is too thick, stir in 2 to 4 tablespoons remaining buttermilk. Pour batter by heaping tablespoonfuls onto a well-greased hot griddle. Cook until bubbles appear on the surface; turn and continue cooking until golden. Garnish as desired.

Nutrition Per Serving: 206 calories, 6g fat, 3g sat fat, 57mg cholesterol, 552mg sodium, 30g carbohydrate, 3g fiber, 5g sugars, 8g protein.

Sharon Newell, *Hancock, MI*

Baked Blueberry Oatmeal

This is one of my favorite brunch recipes. It's easy and can be mixed up the night before.

Makes 8 servings

4 c. old-fashioned oats, uncooked
3/4 c. brown sugar
2 t. baking powder
2 c. skim milk
1/2 c. butter, melted and slightly cooled
4 eggs, beaten
3/4 c. unsweetened applesauce
1 c. blueberries, thawed if frozen
Optional: brown sugar

In a large bowl, mix together all ingredients except blueberries and brown sugar. Spoon into a lightly greased 13"x9" baking pan. Add blueberries; push down into mixture. If desired, sprinkle brown sugar on top. Bake, uncovered, at 350 degrees for 40 minutes, or until golden.

Nutrition Per Serving: 411 calories, 17g fat, 9g sat fat, 125mg cholesterol, 194mg sodium, 56g carbohydrate, 5g fiber, 28g sugars, 11g protein.

Kelly Patrick, *Ashburn, VA*

Mom's Best Orange Muffins

This recipe takes me back to my younger days when I'd give Mom a call and ask her to make these muffins!

Makes 2 dozen, serves 24

1 1/2 c. golden raisins
2 c. boiling water
1 1/2 c. oat bran
1 c. wheat bran
1 c. all-purpose flour
1 c. ground flax seed
1 T. baking powder
1/2 t. salt
2 oranges, peeled, quartered and seeds removed
3/4 c. brown sugar, packed
1 c. non-fat buttermilk
1/4 c. canola oil
1/4 c. unsweetened applesauce
2 eggs
1 t. baking soda
Garnish: orange peel, golden raisins

Place raisins in a bowl; cover with boiling water and set aside. Meanwhile, in a separate bowl, mix together oat and wheat bran, flour, flax seed, baking powder and salt; set aside. In a blender, combine remaining ingredients except garnish; process well. Add orange mixture to bran mixture; stir just to moisten. Drain raisins well and pat dry; fold into batter. Spoon batter into 24 paper-lined or greased muffin cups, filling 2/3 full. Bake at 375 degrees for 18 to 20 minutes, until a toothpick inserted in the center tests clean. Garnish as desired.

Nutrition Per Serving: 166 calories, 6g fat, 1g sat fat, 16mg cholesterol, 193mg sodium, 28g carbohydrate, 5g fiber, 14g sugars, 4g protein.

Mom's Best Orange Muffins

Maxine Griffin, *Heber Springs, AR*

Simple Southwest Omelet

This yummy omelet goes together in a jiffy. Try Mexican-blend cheese for extra zest!

Serves 4

2 slices bacon, diced
1 jalapeño pepper, seeded and diced
4 eggs, beaten
salt and pepper to taste
1 c. shredded Cheddar cheese

In a skillet over medium heat, cook bacon until nearly crisp and golden. Add jalapeño pepper and cook until tender. Drain, reserving one tablespoon drippings in skillet. Reduce heat to low; pour eggs over bacon mixture. Cook until almost set, gently lifting up edges with a spatula to let uncooked egg run underneath. When set, sprinkle with cheese; fold omelet in half and cut into wedges.

Nutrition Per Serving: 194 calories, 14g fat, 8g sat fat, 220mg cholesterol, 282mg sodium, 2g carbohydrate, 0g fiber, 0g sugars, 14g protein.

Jody Pressley, *Charlotte, NC*

Bran & Raisin Muffins

These bran muffins are an all-time favorite with just about everyone!

Makes one dozen, serves 12

2 c. bran & raisin cereal
1½ c. skim milk
1½ c. all-purpose flour
1 t. baking soda
¼ t. salt
1 egg, beaten
½ c. brown sugar, packed
2 T. butter, melted

Mix cereal with milk; set aside. In a large bowl, combine remaining ingredients; stir in cereal mixture. Fill lightly greased or paper-lined muffin cups about ⅔ full with batter. Bake at 350 degrees for 20 to 25 minutes.

Nutrition Per Serving: 166 calories, 3g fat, 1g sat fat, 21mg cholesterol, 235mg sodium, 33g carbohydrate, 1g fiber, 16g sugars, 4g protein.

Mary Schrock, *Seaton, IL*

Peanut Butter-Honey Spread

This tastes absolutely great on toast!

Makes 1½ cups, serves 12

¼ c. creamy peanut butter
2 T. butter, softened
½ c. powdered sugar
⅓ c. honey
¼ t. cinnamon

Beat all ingredients together until fluffy. Spoon into an airtight container; cover and keep refrigerated.

Nutrition Per Serving: 93 calories, 5g fat, 2g sat fat, 5mg cholesterol, 26mg sodium, 13g carbohydrate, 0g fiber, 12g sugars, 1g protein.

Peanut Butter-Honey Spread

Spinach Quiche

Terri Scungio, *Williamsburg, VA*

Spinach Quiche

Even if your kids say they don't like spinach, they will love this quiche!

Serves 8

12-oz. pkg. frozen spinach soufflé, thawed
2 eggs, beaten
3 T. 2% milk
2 t. onion, chopped
3/4 c. Italian ground pork sausage, browned
   and drained
1/2 c. sliced mushrooms
3/4 c. low-fat shredded Swiss cheese
9-inch pie crust, baked

In a bowl, mix together all ingredients except crust; pour into crust. Bake at 400 degrees for 30 to 45 minutes, until golden and center is set. Cut into wedges.

Nutrition Per Serving: 213 calories, 13g fat, 4g sat fat, 58mg cholesterol, 351mg sodium, 14g carbohydrate, 2g fiber, 1g sugars, 10g protein.

Kitchen Helper

Prepare all of your ingredients for your quiche the night before and keep refrigerated. Then just pour into the crust in the morning and bake...so easy!

Vickie, *Gooseberry Patch*

Farmers' Market Omelet

I love visiting the farmers' market bright & early on Saturday mornings...a terrific way to begin the day!

Serves 2

1 t. olive oil
1 slice bacon, diced
2 T. onion, chopped
2 T. zucchini, diced
5 cherry tomatoes, quartered
1/4 t. fresh thyme, minced
3 eggs, beaten
1/4 c. fontina cheese, shredded

Heat oil in a skillet over medium-high heat. Add bacon and onion; cook and stir until bacon is crisp and onion is tender. Add zucchini, tomatoes and thyme. Allow to cook until zucchini is soft and juice from tomatoes has slightly evaporated. Lower heat to medium and stir in eggs. Stir eggs around skillet with a spatula to cook evenly. Continue to cook, lifting edges to allow uncooked egg to flow underneath. When eggs are almost fully cooked, sprinkle cheese over top and fold over.

Nutrition Per Serving: 204 calories, 15g fat, 6g sat fat, 297mg cholesterol, 254mg sodium, 4g carbohydrate, 1g fiber, 2g sugars, 14g protein.

Spinach & Tomato French Toast

Linda Bonwill. *Englewood, FL*

Spinach & Tomato French Toast

A healthier way to make French toast...plus, it looks so pretty!

Serves 4

3 eggs
salt and pepper to taste
8 slices Italian bread
4 c. fresh spinach, torn
2 tomatoes, sliced
shaved Parmesan cheese

In a bowl, beat eggs with salt and pepper. Dip bread slices into egg. Place in a lightly greased skillet over medium heat; cook one side until lightly golden. Place fresh spinach, tomato slice and cheese onto each slice, pressing lightly to secure. Flip and briefly cook on other side until cooked. Flip over and serve open-face.

Nutrition Per Serving: 235 calories, 6g fat, 2g sat fat, 137mg cholesterol, 442mg sodium, 34g carbohydrate, 3g fiber, 3g sugars, 11g protein.

> ### ∼ Healthy Fact ∼
> Whether you call it a fruit or a veggie, tomatoes are the major dietary source of the antioxidant lycopene, which has been linked to many health benefits. Tomatoes are also a great source of potassium, folate and vitamins C and K.

Flo Burtnett, *Gage, OK*

Apple-Raisin Muffins

The chopped apple in these muffins keeps them very moist. They also have a wonderfully spicy flavor that we love.

Makes one dozen, serves 12

1 egg
¾ c. skim milk
1 c. raisins
1 apple, peeled, cored and shredded
½ c. oil
1 c. all-purpose flour
1 c. quick-cooking oats, uncooked
⅓ c. sugar
1 T. baking powder
1 t. salt
1 t. nutmeg
2 t. cinnamon
Garnish: butter

Whisk egg in a bowl; stir in remaining ingredients, except garnish, just until moistened. Mixture will be lumpy. Fill 12 greased or paper-lined muffin cups ¾ full. Bake at 400 degrees for 15 to 20 minutes. Serve warm, topped with butter.

Nutrition Per Serving: 245 calories, 11g fat, 1g sat fat, 16mg cholesterol, 212mg sodium, 35g carbohydrate, 2g fiber, 15g sugars, 5g protein.

Carol Odachowski, *Wakefield, MA*

Carol's Famous Pancakes

These pancakes are so delicious, you will want to double the recipe to make plenty of extras for everyone!

Serves 4

1 egg, beaten
²/₃ c. 2% milk
¼ c. oil
1 c. all-purpose flour
2 t. baking powder
¼ t. baking soda
½ c. powdered sugar

Combine egg, milk and oil in a bowl; sift together remaining ingredients and stir into egg mixture until well blended. Pour by ¼ cupfuls onto a lightly greased hot griddle. Cook until bubbles appear on the surface; turn and continue cooking for an additional 2 to 3 minutes.

Nutrition Per Serving: 322 calories, 16g fat, 2g sat fat, 50mg cholesterol, 360mg sodium, 39g carbohydrate, 1g fiber, 14g sugars, 6g protein.

Happy Presentation

Make breakfast even more fun for the kids by pouring the pancake batter into unexpected shapes such as flowers or animal shapes.

Meri Herbert, *Cheboygan, MI*

Carroty Bran Muffins

These muffins are filled with all kinds of goodness for your family. Your entire family will love them and you'll know they are so good for them!

Makes 16 large muffins, serves 16

2½ c. all-purpose flour
2½ c. bran cereal
1½ c. sugar
2½ t. baking soda
1 t. salt
2 c. buttermilk
⅓ c. applesauce
2 eggs, beaten
1½ c. carrots, peeled and shredded
1 green apple, cored and chopped
1 c. sweetened dried cranberries
½ c. chopped walnuts
¼ c. ground flax seed

Mix all ingredients together in a large bowl. Cover and refrigerate batter for up to 2 days, or bake right away. Fill 16 large, greased muffin cups ²/₃ full. Bake at 375 degrees for 15 to 18 minutes; do not overbake. Muffins will become moister if allowed to stand for awhile.

Nutrition Per Serving: 263 calories, 4g fat, 1g sat fat, 24mg cholesterol, 440mg sodium, 53g carbohydrate, 5g fiber, 30g sugars, 6g protein.

Carroty Bran Muffins

Chapter Two

Light & Lively Lunch

Do lunch right with **Salads, Sandwiches & Pizzas** that give healthy energy for the rest of the day. Garden-Fresh Pesto Pizza makes an easy grab-and-go lunch for a busy family. Love your burgers? Key West Burgers are a new twist on an all-time favorite, adding fresh cilantro, lime juice and a slice of mango. Cranberry-Gorgonzola Green Salad is the perfect light lunch to enjoy with a fresh muffin or whole-grain toast. Whatever you choose to make for lunch, you'll find a recipe that you know is fun to make and good for you!

All-American Sandwiches

Jo Ann, *Gooseberry Patch*

All-American Sandwiches

So simple to make yet so satisfying, these yummy turkey sandwiches are aways a hit at our house!

Serves 4

1½ T. olive oil
1 red onion, thinly sliced
3½ T. red wine vinegar
6 c. fresh arugula leaves, divided
¼ c. low-fat mayonnaise
salt and pepper to taste
4 small whole-grain ciabatta rolls, halved
½ lb. thinly sliced reduced-sodium smoked
    deli turkey
¼ c. crumbled blue cheese

Heat oil in a skillet over medium-high heat. Add onion and sauté until soft and lightly golden. Remove from heat and stir in vinegar. Set aside. Chop enough arugula to equal one cup. Stir in mayonnaise; season with salt and pepper. Spread arugula mixture over cut sides of rolls. Divide turkey evenly among bottom halves of rolls. Top with cheese, onion mixture, remaining arugula leaves and top halves of rolls.

Nutrition Per Serving: 276 calories, 13g fat, 3g sat fat, 34mg cholesterol, 826mg sodium, 23g carbohydrate, 4g fiber, 7g sugars, 18g protein.

Mary Bettuchy, *Columbia, SC*

Orzo with Basil & Prosciutto

If you prefer not to add wine, the step where it's added and simmered can be omitted. Simply skip ahead to the next step, adding one cup of broth.

Serves 6

3 shallots, diced
3 cloves garlic, minced
2 T. olive oil, divided
4 thin slices prosciutto, cut into ½-inch pieces
¾ c. white wine
¾ c. low-sodium chicken broth
juice of one lemon
10 fresh basil leaves, chopped
16-oz. pkg. orzo pasta, cooked
¼ c. shredded Parmigiano-Reggiano cheese

In a skillet over medium-high heat, sauté shallots and garlic in one tablespoon oil for 3 to 4 minutes. Reduce heat to medium; add prosciutto and sauté one minute. Add wine and reduce heat to low. Simmer until most of liquid evaporates. Increase heat to medium; add broth, juice and basil. Stir to combine. Simmer for about 5 minutes. Add orzo and continue to simmer about 2 minutes, or until most of the liquid has evaporated. Drizzle with remaining oil and sprinkle with cheese. Stir to combine.

Nutrition Per Serving: 393 calories, 7g fat, 2g sat fat, 12mg cholesterol, 335mg sodium, 64g carbohydrate, 2g fiber, 1g sugars, 10g protein.

Geneva Rogers, *Gillette, WY*

Aunt Betty's Sandwiches

As kids, our summertime drive to Aunt Betty's was a long-awaited treat. We always looked forward to these sandwiches.

Serves 4

4 ciabatta rolls
3 T. olive oil, divided, plus more for drizzling
whole-grain mustard to taste
1 cup fontina cheese, shredded and divided
12-oz. pkg. sliced mushrooms
2 T. shallots, chopped
3 cloves garlic, pressed
2 chicken breasts, cooked and shredded
5-oz. pkg. baby spinach

Slice tops from rolls; set aside. Hollow out each roll; drizzle inside of each with oil. Spread inside of each roll with mustard; sprinkle with half the cheese. Heat 2 tablespoons remaining oil in a skillet over medium-high heat. Add mushrooms; sauté until tender. Stir in shallots and garlic; cook and stir about 3 minutes. Add chicken; continue cooking until heated through. Transfer to a plate and keep warm. Add remaining oil to skillet. Stir in spinach and season with salt and pepper. Cook about 2 minutes; drain. Spoon chicken mixture into rolls; top with spinach. Sprinkle each with remaining cheese. Cover with tops of rolls and wrap each tightly in aluminum foil. Bake at 400 degrees about 20 minutes, or until cheese is melted.

Nutrition Per Serving: 441 calories, 23g fat, 7g sat fat, 59mg cholesterol, 633mg sodium, 36g carbohydrate, 3g fiber, 4g sugars, 25g protein.

Jo Ann, *Gooseberry Patch*

Aloha Burgers

The grilled pineapple on these sandwiches makes them extra special!

Serves 4

8-oz. can pineapple slices, drained and
    juice reserved
3/4 c. low-sodium teriyaki sauce
1 lb. ground turkey
1 T. butter, softened
4 wheat sandwich thins, split
2 slices Swiss cheese, halved
4 slices reduced-sodium bacon, crisply cooked
4 leaves lettuce
1 red onion, sliced

Stir together reserved pineapple juice and teriyaki sauce in a small bowl. Place pineapple slices and 3 tablespoons juice mixture into a plastic zipping bag. Turn to coat; set aside. Shape ground turkey into 4 patties and spoon remaining juice mixture over top; set aside. Spread butter on buns; set aside. Grill patties over medium-high heat until well done, turning to cook on both sides. Place buns on grill, cut-side down, to toast lightly. Remove pineapple slices from plastic bag; place on grill and heat through until lightly golden, about one minute per side. Serve burgers on buns topped with pineapple, cheese, bacon, lettuce and onion.

Nutrition Per Serving: 419 calories, 20g total fat, 8g sat fat, 111mg cholesterol, 480mg sodium, 32g carbohydrate, 20g sugars, 7g fiber, 31g protein.

Aloha Burgers

Linda Stone, *Cookeville, TN*

Dilled New Potato Salad

The red potatoes in this salad make it so pretty!

Serves 8

2 lbs. redskin potatoes, cut into wedges
10-oz. pkg. frozen petite sweet peas
$\frac{1}{2}$ c. light mayonnaise
$\frac{1}{2}$ c. plain yogurt
1 sweet onion, chopped
$\frac{1}{2}$ t. garlic salt
$\frac{1}{4}$ t. pepper
3 T. fresh dill, minced
1 T. Dijon mustard

In a saucepan over medium-high heat, cover potatoes with water. Cook for 15 minutes, or until nearly tender. Add peas and cook for an additional 2 minutes. Drain potatoes and peas. Cool slightly. In a large bowl, stir together remaining ingredients. Add potato mixture; toss gently to coat. Cover and chill at least 2 hours.

Nutrition Per Serving: 161 calories, 4g fat, 1g sat fat, 3mg cholesterol, 277mg sodium, 27g carbohydrate, 4g fiber, 5g sugars, 5g protein.

Lori Rosenberg, *University Heights, OH*

Waldorf Slaw

This is a variation of the famous Waldorf salad that has been enjoyed for years. We made it into a slaw and we love to serve it with grilled salmon or burgers.

Makes 10 servings

16-oz. pkg. coleslaw mix
2 c. Braeburn apples, peeled, cored, and chopped
1 c. Bartlett pears, peeled, cored, and chopped
$\frac{1}{2}$ c. raisins
3 T. chopped walnuts
$\frac{1}{2}$ c. light mayonnaise
$\frac{1}{2}$ c. low-fat buttermilk
1 t. lemon zest
2 T. lemon juice
$\frac{1}{4}$ t. salt
$\frac{1}{8}$ t. pepper

Combine coleslaw, apples, pears, raisins and walnuts in a large bowl; set aside. Combine remaining ingredients, stirring well with a whisk. Drizzle mayonnaise mixture over coleslaw mixture and toss to coat. Cover and refrigerate 30 minutes.

Nutrition Per Serving: 100 calories, 4g fat, 1g sat fat, 2mg cholesterol, 191mg sodium, 16g carbohydrate, 2g fiber, 10g sugars, 2g protein.

Carolyn Ayers, *Kent, WA*

Chinese Coleslaw

Crunchy, colorful and full of flavor, but it's the dressing that really makes this a stand-out!

Makes 12 servings

9 c. Napa cabbage, shredded
4 c. green cabbage, shredded
1 c. red or green pepper, sliced
1 c. snow pea pods
1 c. bean sprouts
5 green onions, sliced
Garnish: 2 T. toasted sesame seed

Combine vegetables in a large bowl. Drizzle with Sesame-Ginger Dressing; toss and sprinkle with sesame seed. Toss once more before serving.

SESAME-GINGER DRESSING:

1 clove garlic, minced
$1/8$-inch-thick slice fresh ginger, peeled
   and minced
$1/4$ c. sesame seed oil or peanut oil
3 T. soy sauce
3 T. rice wine vinegar
1 t. sugar
Optional: 4 drops chili oil

Combine all ingredients in a jar with a tight-fitting lid. Secure lid and shake well to blend.

Nutrition Per Serving: 60 calories, 4g fat, 0g sat fat, 0mg cholesterol, 19mg sodium, 6g carbohydrate, 2g fiber, 4g sugars, 2g protein.

Amber Sutton, *Naches, WA*

Cherry Tomato Hummus Wraps

I love those little tomatoes that you can eat like candy straight from the vine...especially in a wrap!

Makes 4 servings

4 T. hummus
4 8-inch flour tortillas, warmed
1 c. cherry tomatoes, halved
$1/2$ c. Kalamata olives, chopped
$1/3$ c. crumbled feta cheese
6 sprigs fresh basil, snipped

Spread one tablespoon hummus down the center of each tortilla. Divide remaining ingredients evenly over hummus. To wrap up tortillas burrito-style, turn tortillas so that fillings are side-to-side. Fold in left and right sides of each tortilla; fold top and bottom edges over the filling.

Nutrition Per Serving: 223 calories, 9g fat, 3g sat fat, 11mg cholesterol, 613mg sodium, 29g carbohydrate, 3g fiber, 4g sugars, 7g protein.

JoAnna Nicoline-Haughey, *Berwyn, PA*

English Muffin Pizzas

Back in the 1960s when I was growing up, my mom used to make these for us as an after-school snack. Add some pepperoni slices or other favorite toppings, if you like.

Makes 6 servings

12-oz. pkg. English muffins, split
15-oz. can pizza sauce
1 c. shredded low-fat mozzarella cheese

Spread each muffin half with pizza sauce; sprinkle with cheese. Bake at 350 degrees for 10 minutes, or until cheese is melted.

Nutrition Per Serving: 225 calories, 6g fat, 3g sat fat, 12mg cholesterol, 496mg sodium, 32g carbohydrate, 3g fiber, 3g sugars, 11g protein.

Kim Hinshaw, *Austin, TX*

Turkey & Berry Sandwiches

I served these sandwiches to friends while we were vacationing at the beach. Everyone raved and requested the recipe!

Serves 2

2 lettuce leaves
2 slices Swiss cheese
1/4 lb. thinly sliced low-sodium deli turkey
4 strawberries, hulled and sliced

4 slices thinly-sliced whole-wheat bread
2 T. whipped cream cheese spread
2 t. pecans, finely chopped

Layer lettuce, cheese, turkey and strawberries on 2 slices of bread. Combine cream cheese and pecans. Spread over remaining bread slices; close sandwiches.

Nutrition Per Serving: 351 calories, 9g fat, 3g sat fat, 43mg cholesterol, 810mg sodium, 41g carbohydrate, 5g fiber, 7g sugars, 28g protein.

Crystal Bruns, *Iliff, CO*

Avocado Egg Salad Sandwiches

A fresh and delicious twist on egg salad... serve it on your favorite hearty bread!

Makes 6 sandwiches, serves 6

6 eggs, hard-boiled, peeled and chopped
2 avocados, halved, pitted and cubed
1/4 c. red onion, minced
1/3 c. mayonnaise
1 T. mustard
salt and pepper to taste
12 slices thinly-sliced whole-grain bread

Mash eggs with a fork in a bowl until crumbly. Add remaining ingredients except bread slices. Gently mix together until blended. Spread egg mixture evenly over 6 bread slices. Top with remaining bread slices.

Nutrition Per Serving: 327 calories, 18g fat, 4g sat fat, 189mg cholesterol, 423mg sodium, 29g carbohydrate, 7g fiber, 5g sugars, 14g protein.

Avocado Egg Salad Sandwiches

Chicken Taco Salad

Abby Snay, *San Francisco, CA*

Chicken Taco Salad

Making your own taco salad holder for this salad is part of the special presentation for this dish. It is so fun and easy!

Makes 8 servings

8 6-inch flour tortillas
2 c. cooked chicken breast, shredded
2 t. low-sodium taco seasoning mix
$1/2$ c. water
2 c. lettuce, shredded
$1/2$ c. low-sodium black beans, drained
　　and rinsed
1 c. shredded low-fat Cheddar cheese
$1/2$ c. green onion, sliced
$1/2$ c. canned corn, drained
$2^{1}/_{4}$-oz. can sliced black olives, drained
$1/2$ avocado, pitted, peeled and cubed
Garnish: fresh salsa

Microwave tortillas on high setting for one minute, or until softened. Press each tortilla into an ungreased muffin cup to form a bowl shape. Bake at 350 degrees for 10 minutes; cool. Combine chicken, taco seasoning and water in a skillet over medium heat. Cook, stirring frequently, until blended, about 5 minutes. Divide lettuce among tortilla bowls. Top with chicken and other ingredients, garnishing with salsa.

Nutrition Per Serving: 223 calories, 7g fat, 2g sat fat, 33mg cholesterol, 505mg sodium, 22g carbohydrate, 3g fiber, 2g sugars, 18g protein.

Karen Congeni, *Bath, OH*

Shealeen's Black Bean Salad

My friend Shealeen got this recipe from a friend who lives in Venezuela. I have modified it over the years. It's delicious and versatile, and I get requests for it everywhere I take it. It may be enjoyed as either a salad or a dip for crunchy tortilla chips.

Makes 15 servings

3 15-oz. cans black beans, drained and rinsed
15-oz. can light red kidney beans, drained and
　　rinsed
10-oz. pkg. frozen corn, thawed
1 red onion, chopped
3 to 4 jalapeño peppers, diced
3 to 4 cloves garlic, pressed
$1/2$ c. red wine vinegar
$1/4$ c. olive oil
$1/2$ t. ground cumin
salt and pepper to taste
1 bunch fresh cilantro, chopped

In a large serving bowl, mix together all ingredients. Cover and refrigerate until serving time. If making ahead of time, mix all ingredients except cilantro; sprinkle cilantro on top of salad. Just before serving, stir in cilantro. Will keep for several days in the refrigerator.

Nutrition Per Serving: 167 calories, 4g fat, 1g sat fat, 0mg cholesterol, 179mg sodium, 25g carbohydrate, 9g fiber, 1g sugars, 8g protein.

Beckie Kreml, *Peebles, OH*

Good Times Veggie Pizza

My mom used to make this quick pizza for our church's fellowship on Sundays after the evening service. Try cutting your pizza into bite-size squares for easy nibbling.

Makes 16 servings

2 8-oz. tubes refrigerated crescent rolls
8-oz. pkg. light cream cheese, softened
1 t. dried oregano
1 t. dried basil
1 c. broccoli, finely chopped
1 c. carrots, peeled and diced
1 c. green peppers, diced
½ c. tomatoes, diced
½ c. lettuce, chopped
1 c. shredded Cheddar cheese

Roll out crescent roll dough onto an ungreased baking sheet. Press seams together to form a rectangle. Pinch together edges to form a crust. Bake at 375 minutes for 12 minutes; cool completely. Combine cream cheese and herbs. Spread over crust; top with vegetables, then shredded cheese. Cover and refrigerate for at least an hour; cut into squares.

Nutrition Per Serving: 157 calories, 8g fat, 4g sat fat, 15mg cholesterol, 402mg sodium, 15g carbohydrate, 1g fiber, 2g sugars, 5g protein.

Georgia Cooper, *Helena, MT*

Cranberry-Gorgonzola Green Salad

I love to serve this salad on hot summer days...it is so refreshing and easy to make.

Serves 8

⅓ c. oil
¼ c. seasoned rice vinegar
¾ t. Dijon mustard
1 clove garlic, pressed
1 small head Bibb lettuce, torn
1 small head green leaf lettuce, torn
1 red apple, cored and chopped
⅓ c. coarsely chopped walnuts, toasted
⅓ c. dried cranberries
⅓ c. crumbled Gorgonzola cheese

Whisk together first 4 ingredients in a small bowl; set aside. Just before serving, combine remaining ingredients in a large bowl. Pour dressing over salad; toss gently.

Nutrition Per Serving: 175 calories, 14g fat, 2g sat fat, 4mg cholesterol, 209mg sodium, 11g carbohydrate, 2g fiber, 8g sugars, 3g protein.

Cranberry-Gorgonzola Green Salad

Rebecca Billington, *Birmingham, AL*

Dilly Chicken Sandwiches

This is a great sandwich to make for a family get-together. We always add several bread & butter pickles to our sandwiches...we think they make the sandwich taste even better!

Makes 4 servings

4 boneless, skinless chicken breasts
4 T. butter, softened and divided
1 clove garlic, minced
3/4 t. dill weed, divided
8 slices thinly sliced French bread
4 T. light cream cheese, softened
2 t. lemon juice
Garnish: lettuce leaves, tomato slices,
    bread & butter pickles

Place one chicken breast between 2 pieces of wax paper. Using a mallet, flatten to 1/4-inch thickness. Repeat with remaining chicken; set aside. In a skillet over medium-high heat, melt 3 tablespoons butter; stir in garlic and 1/2 teaspoon dill weed. Add chicken; cook on both sides until juices run clear. Remove and keep warm. Spread both sides of bread with remaining butter. In a skillet or griddle, grill bread on both sides until golden. Combine cream cheese and lemon juice; spread on one side of 4 slices grilled bread. Top with chicken; garnish as desired. Top with remaining bread.

Nutrition Per Serving: 410 calories, 18g fat, 9g sat fat, 93mg cholesterol, 635mg sodium, 38g carbohydrate, 2g fiber, 3g sugars, 26g protein.

Jennifer Oglesby, *Brookville, IN*

Garden-Fresh Pesto Pizza

With this easy pizza, you can really taste what summer is all about! I came up with this recipe last summer when I had a bounty of cherry tomatoes and fresh basil.

Makes 8 servings

12-inch pizza crust
1/3 c. basil pesto
1/2 c. shredded low-fat mozzarella cheese
1 1/2 c. cherry tomatoes, halved
Optional: 4 leaves fresh basil

Place crust on a 12" pizza pan, lightly greased with non-stick vegetable spray if directed on package. Spread pesto over pizza crust and top with cheese. Scatter tomatoes over cheese; add a basil leaf to each quarter of the pizza, if desired. Bake at 425 degrees for about 8 to 10 minutes, until crust is crisp and cheese is lightly golden. Cut into wedges or squares.

Nutrition Per Serving: 193 calories, 10g fat, 2g sat fat, 6mg cholesterol, 228mg sodium, 19g carbohydrate, 1g fiber, 1g sugars, 6g protein.

Kitchen Helper

Chop fresh herbs and keep in small plastic bags in the freezer to have handy for busy cooking days.

Garden-Fresh Pesto Pizza

Mediterranean Salad

Shirl Parsons, *Cape Carteret, NC*

Mediterranean Salad

This fresh and filling salad is perfect for a light lunch. I like to serve it with crackers or whole-grain toast.

Makes 6 servings

4 boneless, skinless chicken breasts
1 T. fresh basil, chopped
¼ t. salt
¼ t. pepper
1 c. cucumber, chopped
½ c. carrot, peeled and shredded
¼ c. celery, diced
½ c. light mayonnaise
¼ c. roasted red pepper, chopped
¼ c. sliced black olives
¼ c. plain yogurt
¼ t. garlic powder
lettuce leaves
Garnish: sliced cucumber, sliced cherry
    tomatoes

Sauté chicken, basil, salt and pepper in a skillet sprayed with non-stick vegetable spray. Cover with water and bring to a boil. Reduce heat and simmer, covered, 10 to 12 minutes until chicken is no longer pink in center. Remove chicken from pan; set aside to cool. Cube chicken and combine with remaining ingredients except garnish. Toss well to coat. Place chicken salad mixture on lettuce leaves. Garnish as desired.

Nutrition Per Serving: 412 calories, 11g fat, 2g sat fat, 180mg cholesterol, 490mg sodium, 5g carbohydrate, 1g fiber, 2g sugars, 70g protein.

Deborah Lomax, *Peoria, IL*

Raspberry-Dijon Baguettes

A friend shared a similar recipe using roast beef...this is my spin on that recipe using grilled chicken.

Serves 4

1 baguette, sliced
1 T. Dijon mustard
1 T. raspberry jam
4 boneless, skinless chicken breasts, grilled
    and sliced
2 c. arugula leaves
Optional: red onion slices

Spread 4 slices of baguette with mustard. Top remaining slices with raspberry jam. Arrange a layer of grilled chicken over mustard; top with arugula and onion, if desired. Top with remaining baguette slices.

Nutrition Per Serving: 293 calories, 4g fat, 1g sat fat, 54mg cholesterol, 609mg sodium, 40g carbohydrate, 2g fiber, 4g sugars, 25g protein.

Happy Presentation

Choose wood cutting boards to use as serving trays to present your sandwiches. Place a sheet of natural parchment paper under each sandwich.

Vickie, *Gooseberry Patch*

Minty Melon Salad

The spicy, fresh mint really brings out the sweetness of the juicy melon in this bright & cheery salad.

Serves 10

1 c. water
³/₄ c. sugar
3 T. lime juice
1¹/₂ t. fresh mint, chopped
5 c. watermelon, cubed
3 c. cantaloupe, cubed
3 c. honeydew, cubed
2 c. nectarines, pitted and sliced
1 c. blueberries
Garnish: fresh mint sprigs

Combine water, sugar, juice and mint in a saucepan; bring to a boil. Boil for 2 minutes, stirring constantly. Remove from heat; cover and cool completely. Combine fruit in a large bowl. Pour cooled dressing over fruit; stir until well coated. Cover and chill for at least 2 hours, stirring occasionally. Drain liquid before serving. Garnish with fresh mint sprigs.

Nutrition Per Serving: 138 calories, 0g fat, 0g sat fat, 0mg cholesterol, 19mg sodium, 35g carbohydrate, 2g fiber, 31g sugars, 2g protein.

Irene Robinson, *Cincinnati, OH*

Irene's Portabella Burgers

Scrumptious...I promise you won't miss the meat! Serve this on pretzel buns to bring out the beauty of the mushrooms.

Serves 4

4 portabella mushroom caps
1 c. Italian salad dressing
4 pretzel or sourdough buns, split
4 slices Muenster or Gruyère cheese
Garnish: romaine lettuce or arugula

Combine mushrooms and salad dressing in a plastic zipping bag, turning to coat. Chill 30 minutes, turning occasionally. Remove mushrooms, discarding dressing. Grill mushrooms, covered with grill lid, over medium heat for 2 to 3 minutes on each side. Grill buns, cut-side down, one minute, or until toasted. Top buns with mushroom, cheese and lettuce or arugula; serve sandwiches immediately.

Nutrition Per Serving: 243 calories, 11g fat, 5g sat fat, 22mg cholesterol, 486mg sodium, 26g carbohydrate, 2g fiber, 6g sugars, 11g protein.

Irene's Portabella Burgers

Amy Gerhart, *Farmington, MI*

Mother's Cucumber Salad

This is my mother's recipe...it always reminds me of summer and picnics. Cool, crisp, not to mention delicious, it tastes even better the longer it marinates in the refrigerator.

Serves 6

3 to 4 cucumbers, peeled and thinly sliced
3 T. salt
2 T. sugar
½ t. onion powder
¼ t. celery seed
¼ t. pepper
¼ c. cider vinegar
Optional: ½ c. sliced red onion

Place cucumbers in a large bowl; add salt and enough water to cover. Cover and shake to combine. Refrigerate several hours to overnight. Drain cucumbers, but do not rinse; return to bowl. Stir together sugar, onion powder, celery seed, pepper and vinegar in a small bowl; mix well. Pour vinegar mixture over cucumbers. Add onion, if desired. Cover and shake gently to mix.

Nutrition Per Serving: 26 calories, 0g fat, 0g sat fat, 0mg cholesterol, 789mg sodium, 5g carbohydrate, 1g fiber, 4g sugars, 1g protein.

Sister Toni Spencer, *Watertown, SD*

Sunflower Strawberry Salad

A great chilled salad...one of our favorite for hot summer days!

Serves 6

2 c. strawberries, hulled and sliced
1 apple, cored and diced
1 c. seedless green grapes, halved
½ c. celery, thinly sliced
¼ c. raisins
½ c. strawberry yogurt
2 T. sunflower seed kernels
Optional: lettuce leaves

Combine fruit, celery and raisins. Stir in yogurt. Cover and chill one hour. Sprinkle with sunflower seeds just before serving. Spoon servings over lettuce leaves, if desired.

Nutrition Per Serving: 107 calories, 2g fat, 0g sat fat, 1mg cholesterol, 21mg sodium, 23g carbohydrate, 3g fiber, 18g sugars, 2g protein.

JoAnne Fajack, *Youngstown, OH*

Bountiful Garden Salad

Grandma always served this salad when we came to visit. We loved to watch her putting it together.

Makes 8 servings

6 c. spinach, torn
1 lb. romaine lettuce, torn
1 stalk celery, chopped
1 red onion, chopped
1 tomato, chopped
$^1/_2$ cucumber, chopped
1 bunch fresh cilantro, chopped
1 clove garlic, finely chopped
$^1/_2$ orange, peeled and sectioned
$^3/_4$ c. blackberries, raspberries and/or
　 blueberries
$^1/_4$ c. strawberries, hulled and sliced
$^1/_4$ c. chopped walnuts, toasted
Raspberry Dressing
Garnish: croutons

Place all ingredients except croutons in a large salad bowl and toss to mix. Drizzle with Raspberry Dressing; garnish with croutons.

RASPBERRY DRESSING:

1 c. raspberries, crushed
3 T. raspberry vinegar
1 T. sugar
2 T. lemon juice
$^1/_4$ t. pepper
$^1/_4$ c. olive oil

Combine raspberries, vinegar, sugar and juice and pepper; slowly drizzle in oil, whisking constantly to blend.

Nutrition Per Serving: 139 calories, 10g fat, 1g sat fat, 0mg cholesterol, 28mg sodium, 13g carbohydrate, 4g fiber, 6g sugars, 3g protein.

Beth Flack, *Terre Haute, IN*

Caprese Salad

Very refreshing! This is one of my favorite summer salads.

Serves 6

2 beefsteak tomatoes, sliced
4-oz. pkg. fresh mozzarella cheese, sliced
8 leaves fresh basil
Italian salad dressing to taste

Layer tomatoes, cheese slices and basil leaves in rows or in a circle around a large platter. Sprinkle with salad dressing. Cover and chill for one hour before serving.

Nutrition Per Serving: 72 calories, 4g fat, 3g sat fat, 15mg cholesterol, 123mg sodium, 4g carbohydrate, 1g fiber, 2g sugars, 5g protein.

Apple-Pomegranate Salad

Wendy Ball, *Battle Creek, MI*

Apple-Pomegranate Salad

This recipe brings back memories of my grandparents, who were fruit growers in California. They would send us fresh-picked pomegranates and wonderful pecans.

Makes 6 servings

1 apple, peeled, cored and diced
juice of 1/2 lemon
1 head romaine lettuce, torn
seeds of 1 pomegranate
1/4 c. chopped pecans
2 T. champagne vinegar or white wine vinegar
2 T. canola oil
1 T. sugar
salt to taste
1/4 c. shredded Parmesan cheese

In a small bowl, toss apple with lemon juice. Let stand for several minutes; rinse apple and pat dry. In a large serving bowl, combine apple, lettuce, pomegranate seeds and nuts. In a small jar, combine vinegar, oil, sugar and salt. Cover jar and shake thoroughly to mix; pour over salad. Toss until lettuce is completely coated; sprinkle with cheese.

Nutrition Per Serving: 164 calories, 10g fat, 1g sat fat, 2mg cholesterol, 116mg sodium, 18g carbohydrate, 5g fiber, 13g sugars, 4g protein.

Diane Chaney, *Olathe, KS*

Crisp Vegetable Salad Medley

A yummy, colorful make-ahead that feeds a crowd...just right for your next family reunion picnic.

Makes 14 servings

2 c. green beans, cut into bite-size pieces
1 1/2 c. peas
1 1/2 c. corn
1 c. cauliflower, cut into bite-size pieces
1 c. celery, chopped
1 c. red onion, chopped
1 c. red pepper, chopped
15-oz. can garbanzo beans, drained and rinsed
4-oz. jar diced pimentos, drained
2 2 1/4-oz. cans sliced black olives, drained

In a large bowl, combine all ingredients. Add dressing and toss to coat. Cover and refrigerate for several hours to overnight, stirring occasionally. Serve with a slotted spoon.

DRESSING:

1 c. sugar
3/4 c. red wine vinegar
1/2 c. oil
1 t. salt
1/2 t. pepper

Whisk ingredients together in a small saucepan. Bring to a boil over medium heat; cool.

Nutrition Per Serving: 193 calories, 9g fat, 1g sat fat, 0mg cholesterol, 270mg sodium, 26g carbohydrate, 3g fiber, 18g sugars, 3g protein.

Evan Mickley, *Delaware, OH*

Grandma Bev's Greek Salad

Whenever Mom makes a salad, my sisters Emma and Gracie and I always ask..."Is this Grandma Bev's Salad?" It's the best!

Makes 6 servings

1/2 c. canola oil
1/4 c. cider vinegar
1 1/2 t. dried oregano
1 1/2 t. garlic powder
1 1/2 t. salt
1 head romaine lettuce, torn
1/2 cucumber, cubed
1/2 c. grape tomatoes, halved
1/4 red onion, thinly sliced
Optional: crumbled feta cheese
Garnish: croutons

Combine oil, vinegar and seasonings in a jar with a tight-fitting lid; shake until thoroughly blended. Set aside. Add remaining ingredients except croutons to a large salad bowl. Toss with dressing to taste; garnish with croutons.

Nutrition Per Serving: 193 calories, 19g fat, 1g sat fat, 0mg cholesterol, 600mg sodium, 6g carbohydrate, 3g fiber, 2g sugars, 2g protein.

Angela Murphy, *Tempe, AZ*

Mom's Homemade Pizza

Nothing is better than homemade pizza!

Makes 10 servings

Pizza Dough
8-oz. can tomato sauce
1/2 t. sugar
1/4 t. pepper
1 t. garlic powder
1 1/2 t. dried thyme
3 T. grated Parmesan cheese
1 onion, finely chopped
5 Roma tomatoes, sliced
1 c. fresh spinach, chopped
1 c. shredded part-skim mozzarella cheese

Prepare Pizza Dough. Combine tomato sauce, sugar and seasonings; spread over dough. Top with Parmesan cheese, onion, tomatoes, spinach and shredded cheese. Bake at 400 degrees for 25 to 30 minutes, until edges are golden.

PIZZA DOUGH:

1 env. quick-rise yeast
1 c. hot water
2 T. olive oil
1/2 t. salt
3 c. all-purpose flour, divided
1 T. cornmeal

Combine yeast and water. Let stand 5 minutes. Add olive oil, salt and half of the flour. Stir to combine. Stir in remaining flour. Gather into a ball and place in oiled bowl. Turn dough over and cover with plastic wrap. Let rise 30 minutes. Brush oil over a 15"x10" jelly-roll pan or 2, 12" round pizza pans; sprinkle with cornmeal. Roll out dough; place on pan.

Nutrition Per Serving: 227 calories, 7g fat, 2g sat fat, 8mg cholesterol, 346mg sodium, 32g carbohydrate, 2g fiber, 3g sugars, 9g protein.

Mom's Homemade Pizza

Janice Pigga, *Bethlehem, PA*

Red Pepper & Chicken Bagels

This is a quick recipe that's perfect whenever time is short.

Serves 2

2 boneless, skinless chicken breasts
1/8 t. pepper
1/4 c. balsamic vinegar
2 T. Worcestershire sauce
2 whole-grain bagel thins, split
2 slices fresh mozzarella cheese
2 slices roasted red pepper

Place chicken between 2 pieces of wax paper; pound until thin. Sprinkle with salt and pepper. In a bowl, combine vinegar and Worcestershire sauce; marinate chicken 10 to 15 minutes. Drain and discard marinade. Place chicken on a lightly greased grill or in a skillet over medium heat. Cook and turn chicken until golden and juices run clear, about 20 minutes. Place chicken on bagel halves; top with cheese, pepper slices and remaining bagel halves. Arrange on an ungreased baking sheet and bake at 350 degrees until cheese is melted, about 5 to 10 minutes.

Nutrition Per Serving: 328 calories, 8g fat, 3g sat fat, 73mg cholesterol, 714mg sodium, 34g carbohydrate, 2g fiber, 10g sugars, 29g protein.

Kimberly Ascroft, *Merritt Island, FL*

Key West Burgers

Dress up a plain burger with a tropical touch using slices of mango and fresh lime juice.

Serves 4

1 lb. lean ground beef
3 T. Key lime juice
1/4 c. fresh cilantro, chopped, divided
salt and pepper to taste
4 whole-wheat hamburger buns, split and
    toasted
Creamy Burger Spread
1 mango, pitted, peeled and sliced
Garnish: lettuce

In a bowl, combine beef, lime juice, 3 tablespoons cilantro, salt and pepper. Form beef mixture into 4 patties. Spray a large skillet with non-stick vegetable spray. Cook patties over medium heat for 6 minutes. Flip patties, cover skillet and cook for another 6 minutes. Place lettuce on bottom halves of buns and top with patties. Add Creamy Burger Spread onto bun tops. Top with mango slices and remaining chopped cilantro. Add bun tops.

CREAMY BURGER SPREAD:

1/2 c. light cream cheese, softened
1/2 c. plain Greek yogurt
3 green onion tops, chopped

Combine all ingredients until completely blended. Cover and refrigerate at least 15 minutes.

Nutrition Per Serving: 390 calories, 14g fat, 7g sat fat, 91mg cholesterol, 494mg sodium, 31g carbohydrate, 3g fiber, 11g sugars, 35g protein.

Key West Burgers

Mix olives, garlic, pimento, herbs, pepper and $\frac{1}{3}$ cup oil in a small bowl; set aside. Cut loaf in half horizontally and hollow out the center. Brush cut side of bottom half with remaining oil; layer ham, turkey and cheese slices on top. Top with pickle slices. Fill top half of loaf with the olive mixture; place bottom loaf on top and invert. Wrap tightly in plastic wrap and chill overnight. Let stand until loaf comes to room temperature; cut into wedges.

Nutrition Per Serving: 261 calories, 19g fat, 4g sat fat, 38mg cholesterol, 702mg sodium, 8g carbohydrate, 1g fiber, 1g sugars, 15g protein.

Kris Bailey, *Conklin, NY*

Muffuletta Sandwich

Layers of flavor and spice make this sandwich an all-time favorite!

Serves 8

$\frac{1}{2}$ c. green olives, chopped
$\frac{1}{2}$ c. black olives, chopped
1 clove garlic, minced
$\frac{1}{3}$ c. chopped pimento
$\frac{1}{4}$ c. fresh parsley, chopped
$\frac{3}{4}$ t. dried oregano
$\frac{1}{4}$ t. pepper
$\frac{1}{3}$ c. plus 1 T. olive oil, divided
1 round loaf Italian bread
$\frac{1}{2}$ lb. sliced low-sodium honey ham
$\frac{1}{2}$ lb. sliced low-sodium turkey
$\frac{1}{4}$ lb. sliced Muenster cheese
4 dill pickle slices, halved

Rebecca Pickett, *Houston, TX*

Summertime Feta & Tomatoes

We love to change up the spices and vinegars in this recipe each time we make it. If you eat all the tomatoes and still have dressing left, dip some crusty bread in it!

Serves 8

7 roma tomatoes, chopped
4-oz. pkg. crumbled feta cheese
$\frac{1}{4}$ c. olive oil
$\frac{1}{2}$ c. red wine vinegar
2 t. Italian seasoning
$\frac{1}{4}$ t. seasoned salt

Combine all ingredients; toss to blend. Refrigerate for 30 minutes to allow flavors to blend.

Nutrition Per Serving: 110 calories, 10g fat, 3g sat fat, 13mg cholesterol, 208mg sodium, 3g carbohydrate, 1g fiber, 2g sugars, 2g protein.

Michael Curry, *Ardmore, OK*

Veggie Delight

I came up with this recipe because I enjoy broccoli slaw so much. I added a few more vegetables and tossed with a tangy Dijon dressing...my family loves it!

Serves 10

16-oz. pkg. shredded cabbage
1 c. carrots, peeled and grated
½ c. broccoli, chopped
½ c. cherry tomatoes, halved
½ c. celery, sliced
½ c. cucumber, peeled and diced
⅓ c. olive oil
2 T. vinegar
1 T. Dijon mustard
1 t. garlic salt

Combine vegetables in a large salad bowl. Whisk together remaining ingredients; drizzle over vegetables. Toss to coat.

Nutrition Per Serving: 86 calories, 7g fat, 1g sat fat, 0mg cholesterol, 229mg sodium, 5g carbohydrate, 2g fiber, 3g sugars, 1g protein.

> ~ **Healthy Fact** ~
>
> There are only 21 calories in one cup of chopped cabbage. Cabbage is also an excellent source of vitamin K, vitamin C and vitamin B6...so enjoy!

LaShelle Brown, *Mulvane, KS*

Rainbow Pasta Salad

This is my husband's all-time favorite pasta salad. It is yummy and pretty!

Serves 8

4 c. rainbow rotini pasta, uncooked
1 cucumber, quartered lengthwise and sliced
1 tomato, chopped
4-oz. can sliced black olives, drained
¾ c. light ranch salad dressing
⅓ c. Italian salad dressing
Optional: shredded Cheddar cheese

Cook pasta according to package directions; drain and rinse with cold water. In a large salad bowl, combine cooked pasta, cucumber, tomato and olives; mix well. In a separate bowl, mix salad dressings together. Add to pasta mixture; toss to coat. Cover and refrigerate for at least one hour.

Nutrition Per Serving: 287 calories, 7g fat, 1g sat fat, 4mg cholesterol, 457mg sodium, 48g carbohydrate, 3g fiber, 4g sugars, 8g protein.

Gennell Williams, *Fieldale, VA*

Guacamole Tossed Salad

This is the ideal salad, no matter the reason for your get-together!

Makes 4 servings

2 tomatoes, chopped
$1/2$ red onion, sliced and separated into rings
4 slices bacon, crisply cooked and crumbled
$1/3$ c. oil
2 T. cider vinegar
$1/4$ t. salt
$1/4$ t. pepper
$1/4$ t. hot pepper sauce
2 avocados, pitted, peeled and cubed
4 c. salad greens, torn

In a bowl, combine tomatoes, onion and bacon. In a separate bowl, whisk together oil, vinegar, salt, pepper and hot pepper sauce. Pour over tomato mixture; toss gently. Add avocados. Place greens in a large serving bowl; add avocado mixture and toss to coat. Serve immediately.

Nutrition Per Serving: 352 calories, 33g fat, 4g sat fat, 11mg cholesterol, 322mg sodium, 11g carbohydrate, 6g fiber, 3g sugars, 6g protein.

Wendy Jacobs, *Idaho Falls, ID*

Grilled Veggie Sandwich

Use any of your favorite freshly picked vegetables for this sandwich!

Makes 10 servings

$1/4$ c. balsamic vinegar
2 T. olive oil
1 T. fresh basil, chopped
1 t. molasses
$1^{1}/2$ t. fresh thyme, chopped
$1/4$ t. pepper
3 zucchini, sliced
$1/2$ yellow pepper, coarsely chopped
2 red peppers, coarsely chopped
1 onion, sliced
16-oz. loaf whole-grain French-style bread
$3/4$ c. crumbled reduced-fat feta cheese
2 T. light mayonnaise
$1/4$ c. freshly grated Parmesan cheese

Whisk together vinegar, olive oil, basil, molasses, thyme, and pepper. Place zucchini, peppers and onion in a large plastic zipping bag. Add vinegar mixture; seal and refrigerate 2 hours, turning bag occasionally. Remove vegetables from bag and set aside; reserve marinade. Slice bread loaf in half horizontally and brush 3 or 4 tablespoons reserved marinade over cut sides of bread. Lightly coat grill pan with non-stick vegetable spray; add vegetables and grill 5 minutes, basting occasionally with remaining marinade. Turn vegetables, baste and grill 2 more minutes. Place bread, cut-sides down on grill and grill 3 minutes or until bread is toasted. Combine feta cheese and mayonnaise; spread evenly over cut sides of bread. Layer grilled vegetables on bread; add Parmesan cheese. Slice into 10 sections.

Nutrition Per Serving: 222 calories, 7g fat, 3g sat fat, 13mg cholesterol, 464mg sodium, 30g carbohydrate, 2g fiber, 4g sugars, 8g protein.

Grilled Veggie Sandwich

Elisha Wiggins, *Suwanee, GA*

Veggie Mini Pizzas

So quick to make, and always a favorite, you will want to make these for your family often!

Serves 6

6 pita rounds or flatbreads
1½ c. pizza or pasta sauce
1 c. baby spinach
1 c. shredded low-fat mozzarella cheese
2 plum tomatoes, sliced

Place pita rounds on an ungreased baking sheet. Spread each with ¼ cup sauce; top with spinach, cheese and tomato. Bake at 350 degrees for 15 to 20 minutes, or until cheese is bubbly.

Nutrition Per Serving: 158 calories, 3g fat, 1g sat fat, 8mg cholesterol, 489mg sodium, 24g carbohydrate, 3g fiber, 4g sugars, 8g protein.

Susan Smith, *London, OH*

Chicken Salad Sandwiches

Served with small slices of fresh melon or strawberries, these sandwiches are perfect for a quick and tasty lunch.

Makes 6 servings

¾ lb. chicken breast, cooked and diced
1 c. celery, thinly sliced
¼ c. seedless red grapes, halved
2½ T. raisins
½ c. plain low-fat yogurt
2 T. light mayonnaise
2 T. shallots, chopped
2 T. fresh tarragon, chopped
⅛ t. salt
⅛ t. white pepper
6 dinner-size whole-wheat buns, split
lettuce leaves

Combine chicken, celery, grapes and raisins in a large bowl. Blend together yogurt, mayonnaise, shallots, tarragon, salt and pepper in a small bowl. Add yogurt mixture to chicken mixture; stir gently to coat. Divide mixture evenly among buns. Place lettuce leaves over chicken mixture and place tops on buns.

Nutrition Per Serving: 249 calories, 5g fat, 1g sat fat, 49mg cholesterol, 385mg sodium, 29g carbohydrate, 4g fiber, 9g sugars, 23g protein.

Anna McMaster, *Portland, OR*

Apricot Chicken Sandwiches

I usually toss grape halves or raisins in my chicken salad, but this is one time I tried something new. It tastes terrific!

Serves 4

4 c. cooked chicken, diced
1 stalk celery, finely diced
2 T. onion, finely chopped
3 apricots, pitted and finely diced
3 T. light mayonnaise
1/8 t. pepper
4 pita rounds, halved

Combine chicken, celery, onion and apricots. Stir in mayonnaise; season to taste. Spoon into pita halves.

Nutrition Per Serving: 355 calories, 8g fat, 2g sat fat, 12mg cholesterol, 362mg sodium, 21g carbohydrate, 2g fiber, 4g sugars, 47g protein.

Pam James, *Delaware, OH*

Picnic Salad Skewers

For a meal-in-one version, slide on some cubes of Cheddar cheese.

Serves 8

8 redskin potatoes
8 pearl onions, peeled
1 green pepper, cut into 1-inch squares
1 red or yellow bell pepper, cut into 1-inch squares
16 cherry tomatoes
1 zucchini, sliced 1/4-inch thick
8 wooden skewers
Vinaigrette
Optional: 4-oz. container crumbled feta cheese

Cover potatoes with water in a saucepan; bring to a boil over medium heat. Cook 10 to 13 minutes, adding onions after 5 minutes; drain and cool. Thread all vegetables alternately onto skewers. Arrange skewers in a large shallow plastic container. Drizzle with Vinaigrette. Cover and refrigerate at least one hour, turning frequently. Sprinkle with cheese before serving, if desired.

VINAIGRETTE:

2/3 c. olive oil
1/3 c. red wine vinegar
2 cloves garlic, minced
1 T. dried oregano
1 t. salt
1/4 t. pepper

Whisk together all ingredients. Makes about one cup.

Nutrition Per Serving: 288 calories, 14g fat, 2g sat fat, 0mg cholesterol, 244mg sodium, 37g carbohydrate, 4g fiber, 4g sugars, 4g protein.

Cheryl Donnelly, *Arvada, CO*

Spinach, Strawberry & Walnut Salad

The colors in this salad are beautiful!

Serves 6

1¹/₂ lbs. spinach, torn
3 c. strawberries, hulled and sliced
1 sweet onion, thinly sliced
³/₄ c. chopped walnuts
Poppy Seed Dressing

Arrange spinach, strawberries, onion and nuts in a salad bowl. Cover and refrigerate. Drizzle desired amount of Poppy Seed Dressing over salad just before serving. Toss and serve immediately.

POPPY SEED DRESSING:

³/₄ c. sugar
1 t. dry mustard
1 t. salt
¹/₃ c. cider vinegar
2 t. green onion, chopped
³/₄ c. olive oil
1¹/₂ T. poppy seed

Place sugar, mustard, salt and vinegar in a blender; cover and blend until smooth. Add onion and blend until smooth. With blender running, add oil slowly. Cover and blend until thick. Stir in poppy seed.

Nutrition Per Serving: 374 calories, 29g fat, 2g sat fat, 0mg cholesterol, 289mg sodium, 26g carbohydrate, 6g fiber, 17g sugars, 8g protein.

Larry Bodner, *Dublin, OH*

Grilled Chicken Salad

The chopped apple in this dressing makes this salad extra special and elegant.

Makes 4 servings

1 c. apple, peeled, cored and finely chopped
¹/₂ c. apple juice
1 T. cider vinegar
1 t. cornstarch
4 boneless, skinless chicken breasts
6-oz. pkg. mixed salad greens
¹/₂ c. red pepper, sliced
³/₄ c. crumbled blue cheese
¹/₂ c. low-fat shredded Cheddar cheese
¹/₄ c. sliced almonds, toasted

Combine apple, juice, vinegar and cornstarch in a small saucepan over medium heat; cook and stir until thickened. Chill. Grill chicken breasts until juices run clear; let cool, then slice. Divide salad greens among 4 serving plates; top each with grilled chicken, red pepper and a sprinkling of cheeses and almonds. Drizzle with dressing and serve immediately.

Nutrition Per Serving: 354 calories, 17g fat, 8g sat fat, 115mg cholesterol, 448mg sodium, 13g carbohydrate, 2g fiber, 8g sugars, 38g protein.

Grilled Chicken Salad

Lisa Schneck, *Lehighton, PA*

Sweet & Savory Beef Sandwiches

This slow-cooker beef sandwich recipe will become a family favorite...so easy!

Serves 8

12-oz. can light beer or non-alcoholic beer
1 c. brown sugar, packed
24-oz. bottle low-sodium catsup
3 to 4-lb. boneless beef roast
8 whole-wheat rolls, split
Optional: banana pepper slices

Stir together beer, sugar and catsup in a slow cooker. Add roast and spoon mixture over top. Cover and cook on low setting for 7 to 8 hours. Remove roast and shred; return to juices in slow cooker. Serve shredded beef on rolls for sandwiches, topped with pepper slices, if desired.

Nutrition Per Serving: 552 calories, 14g fat, 6g sat fat, 137mg cholesterol, 375mg sodium, 65g carbohydrate, 3g fiber, 46g sugars, 45g protein.

> **⚬ Healthy Fact ⚬**
>
> Beef is a source of high-quality protein and nutrients, with about 30 grams of protein in a 4-ounce serving. And it tastes so good in so many ways!

Edie DeSpain, *Logan, UT*

Grilled Salmon BLT's

Lemony dill mayonnaise is the secret ingredient in this oh-so-yummy sandwich.

Serves 4

¼ c. reduced-fat mayonnaise
2 t. fresh dill, chopped
1 t. lemon zest
4 1-inch-thick salmon fillets
⅛ t. pepper
8 ½-inch slices whole-wheat bread
4 romaine lettuce leaves
2 tomatoes, sliced
4 slices bacon, crisply cooked and halved

Stir together mayonnaise, dill and zest; set aside. Sprinkle salmon with salt and pepper; place on a lightly greased hot grill, skin-side down. Cook, covered, about 10 to 12 minutes without turning, until cooked through. Slide a thin metal spatula between salmon and skin; lift salmon and transfer to plate. Discard skin. Arrange bread slices on grill; cook until lightly toasted on both sides. Spread mayonnaise mixture on one side of 4 toasted bread slices. Top each with one lettuce leaf, 2 tomato slices, one salmon fillet, 3 slices bacon and remaining bread slice.

Nutrition Per Serving: 502 calories, 25g fat, 4g sat fat, 52mg cholesterol, 570mg sodium, 50g carbohydrate, 6g fiber, 5g sugars, 28g protein.

Grilled Salmon BLT's

Carol Field Dahlstrom, *Ankeny, IA*

Carol's Sloppy Joes

These quick-to-make sloppy Joes are a much-requested sandwich for a quick lunch.

Serves 8

3 lbs. lean ground beef
1 T. fresh chives, chopped
1 T. fresh parsley, chopped
³/₄ c. low-sodium beef broth
¹/₂ c. catsup
1 T. mustard
¹/₂ c. instant brown rice, uncooked
salt and pepper to taste
8 whole-grain buns, split

Brown ground beef in a skillet with herbs until beef is no longer pink. Transfer to slow cooker and add remaining ingredients except for buns. Mix well. Cover and cook on low setting for 3 to 4 hours. Serve on whole-grain buns.

Nutrition Per Serving: 446 calories, 20g fat, 8g sat fat, 111mg cholesterol, 552mg sodium, 26g carbohydrate, 2g fiber, 6g sugars, 39g protein.

Sherry Rogers, *Stillwater, OK*

Potato Salad for a Crowd

This make-ahead recipe is one that my mother-in-law shared with me. We always prepare it for family reunions and summertime celebrations.

Makes 30 servings

4 c. light mayonnaise-type salad dressing
¹/₄ c. mustard
1 c. sweet pickle relish
¹/₃ c. white vinegar
¹/₄ c. sugar
1 t. salt
7 lbs. potatoes, peeled, cubed and boiled
8 eggs, hard-boiled, peeled and diced
1 yellow onion, finely diced
4-oz. jar diced pimentos, drained

Mix together salad dressing, mustard, relish, vinegar, sugar and seasonings in a very large bowl. Add potatoes; use a potato masher or pastry blender to mash potatoes. Stir in remaining ingredients. Chill before serving.

Nutrition Per Serving: 210 calories, 9g fat, 2g sat fat, 55mg cholesterol, 456mg sodium, 30g carbohydrate, 2g fiber, 7g sugars, 4g protein.

Brenda Huey, *Geneva, IN*

Log Cabin Salad

My mom, Iris, lives in a little log cabin by a lake. I named this salad recipe for her. We love the rice, fruit and greens combination.

Makes 15 servings

2 lbs. salad greens
1/4 lb. bacon, crisply cooked and crumbled
1 c. chopped pecans
6-oz. pkg. long-grain and wild rice, cooked
1 c. crumbled blue cheese
2 1/2 c. blueberries, divided
1 c. favorite poppy seed salad dressing

Arrange greens in a large serving bowl. Toss with bacon, pecans, rice, cheese and 1/2 cup blueberries. Mash remaining blueberries and whisk with salad dressing. Drizzle over individual servings.

Nutrition Per Serving: 323 calories, 23g fat, 5g sat fat, 20mg cholesterol, 572mg sodium, 24g carbohydrate, 3g fiber, 12g sugars, 8g protein.

Phyl Broich Wessling, *Garner, IA*

Fruit & Nut Chicken Salad

I make a double batch of this salad every year for our church's salad luncheon. There are never any leftovers!

Serves 10

4 c. cooked or grilled chicken, diced
11-oz. can mandarin oranges, drained
1 1/2 c. seedless green grapes, halved
1 c. celery, sliced
2-oz. pkg. slivered almonds, lightly toasted
1 c. light mayonnaise
1/4 c. plain Greek yogurt
1/8 t. garlic powder
1/8 t. pepper
Garnish: lettuce leaves

Combine chicken, oranges, grapes, celery and almonds in a large bowl. In another bowl, combine mayonnaise, sour cream and seasonings. Pour mayonnaise mixture over chicken mixture; stir carefully. Cover and chill until serving time. Serve scoops of salad on lettuce leaves.

Nutrition Per Serving: 232 calories, 10g fat, 2g sat fat, 52mg cholesterol, 254mg sodium, 14g carbohydrate, 1g fiber, 11g sugars, 19g protein.

Angie Cornelius, *Sheridan, IL*

Summer in a Bowl

We have a large, wonderful vegetable garden every summer. This salad makes excellent use of all those peppers, cucumbers and tomatoes.

Serves 4

4 roma tomatoes, chopped
1 cubanelle pepper, seeded and chopped
1 cucumber, chopped
¼ c. red onion, minced
6 fresh basil leaves, shredded
salt and pepper to taste
2 c. Italian bread, sliced, cubed and toasted
3 T. olive oil

Combine vegetables, basil, salt and pepper in a bowl. Let stand at room temperature for 30 minutes. At serving time, stir in bread cubes; drizzle with oil. Mix thoroughly; serve at room temperature.

Nutrition Per Serving: 429 calories, 14g fat, 2g sat fat, 0mg cholesterol, 701mg sodium, 64g carbohydrate, 5g fiber, 5g sugars, 11g protein.

Myra Tunanidis, *New Cumberland, WV*

Tangy Summer Slaw

This coleslaw is loaded with fresh flavors...it's a must-try!

Makes 10 servings

1 head red cabbage, shredded
1 head green cabbage, shredded
1 carrot, peeled and shredded
1 onion, finely chopped
1 green pepper, finely chopped
16-oz. bottle red wine vinegar & oil salad
   dressing
¼ c. olive oil
¼ c. sugar
1 T. Dijon mustard
1 t. caraway seed
salt and pepper to taste

Toss together vegetables in a large serving bowl; set aside. Combine remaining ingredients; pour over vegetables. Refrigerate until ready to serve. Toss before serving.

Nutrition Per Serving: 313 calories, 23g fat, 4g sat fat, 0mg cholesterol, 613mg sodium, 23g carbohydrate, 4g fiber, 16g sugars, 3g protein.

Tangy Summer Slaw

Lynda McCormick, *Burkburnett, TX*

Greek Pita Pizzas

These are my healthy go-to summer pizzas. Kids and adults love them! For a crisper crust, spritz pitas with olive oil spray and add a pinch of coarse salt, then broil for one to 2 minutes before adding the toppings.

Makes 8 servings

10-oz. pkg. frozen chopped spinach, thawed
   and well drained
4 green onions, chopped
chopped fresh dill to taste
4 fat-free whole-wheat pita rounds, split
4 roma tomatoes, sliced ½-inch thick
½ c. crumbled feta cheese with basil & tomato
dried oregano or Greek seasoning to taste

Mix spinach, onions and dill in a small bowl. Season with garlic salt and pepper; set aside. Place pita rounds on ungreased baking sheets. Arrange tomato slices among pitas. Spread spinach mixture evenly over tomatoes; spread cheese over tomatoes. Sprinkle with desired seasoning to taste. Bake at 450 degrees for 10 to 15 minutes, until crisp. Cut into wedges.

Nutrition Per Serving: 128 calories, 3g fat, 2g sat fat, 8mg cholesterol, 288mg sodium, 21g carbohydrate, 4g fiber, 2g sugars, 6g protein.

Connie Hilty, *Pearland, TX*

Texas 2-Step Sandwiches

This sandwich is so good, it'll have you doing the Texas 2-step!

Serves 4

1 c. water
½ c. white wine vinegar
1 c. red onion, thinly sliced
1 c. canned low-sodium black beans, drained
   and rinsed
½ t. ground cumin
¼ c. reduced-fat mayonnaise
1 t. canned chipotle chile, finely chopped
1 T. lime juice
4 slices whole-grain bread
⅔ c. crumbled feta cheese
1 avocado, peeled, pitted and thinly sliced
2 T. fresh cilantro, chopped
1 tomato, cut into 8 slices

Pour water into a saucepan; stir in vinegar and onion. Bring to a boil; turn off heat and let stand 30 minutes. Drain. Purée beans and cumin in a blender; set side. Stir together mayonnaise, chile and juice in a bowl; spread on 4 slices of bread. Top with bean purée, onion and remaining ingredients; serve open-faced.

Nutrition Per Serving: 321 calories, 18g fat, 5g sat fat, 27mg cholesterol, 546mg sodium, 29g carbohydrate, 9g fiber, 5g sugars, 12g protein.

Texas 2-Step Sandwiches

Lynda's Salmon Burgers

Lynda McCormick, *Burkburnett, TX*

Lynda's Salmon Burgers

My entire family loves these salmon burgers. I usually serve them with just-picked berries or fresh pineapple.

Makes 8 servings

1 lb. salmon fillet, skin removed and chopped
1/2 c. red onion, finely chopped
1/4 c. fresh basil, thinly sliced
1/4 t. salt
1/4 t. pepper
1 egg white
1 T. sriracha hot chili sauce
Optional: 1/4 c. panko bread crumbs
8 slices whole-grain bread, toasted and cut
   in half
Garnish: lettuce leaves, tomato slices

In a large bowl, combine salmon, onion, basil and seasonings; mix gently. In a small bowl, whisk together egg white and chili sauce. Add to salmon mixture and stir well to combine. If mixture is too soft, stir in bread crumbs if desired. Form mixture into 8 patties. Heat a large non-stick skillet over medium-high heat. Coat pan with non-stick vegetable spray. Add patties to skillet; cook for about 2 to 3 minutes per side. Place patties sandwich-style on toasted wheat bread. Garnish as desired.

Nutrition Per Serving: 193 calories, 9g fat, 2g sat fat, 31mg cholesterol, 187mg sodium, 12g carbohydrate, 2g fiber, 2g sugars, 16g protein.

Madonna Alexander, *Chicago, IL*

Bruschetta Pizza

If you can, prepare the bruschetta mix early in the day. The longer the flavor blends, the better it tastes. You'll have some left over but that's okay. I made an omelet with this mix and it was awesome!

Serves 6

10 roma tomatoes, chopped
5 to 6 cloves garlic, minced
2 T. fresh basil, chopped
1/2 red onion, finely chopped
1/4 c. plus 1 T. olive oil, divided
1/2 t. pepper
1/4 t. garlic salt
1/4 c. balsamic vinegar
13.8-oz. tube refrigerated pizza crust dough
1/2 c. pizza sauce
8-oz. pkg. low-fat shredded Italian-blend
   cheese
dried oregano to taste

In a large bowl, combine tomatoes, garlic, basil, onion, 1/4 cup oil, pepper, garlic salt and vinegar. Stir to blend; drain. Place pizza crust dough on an ungreased baking sheet. Spread with pizza sauce. Top with 1½ to 2 cups tomato mixture. Sprinkle on cheese and oregano. Drizzle remaining oil over top. Bake according to pizza crust dough package directions.

Nutrition Per Serving: 397 calories, 22g fat, 6g sat fat, 21mg cholesterol, 492mg sodium, 35g carbohydrate, 3g fiber, 6g sugars, 15g protein.

Lynda McCormick, *Burkburnett, TX*

Roasted Veggie Panini

No panini press? Place sandwiches on a hot skillet and gently press with a smaller skillet.

Serves 4

2 zucchini, sliced
1 yellow squash, sliced
6 oz. portobello mushroom caps, sliced
2 t. olive oil, divided
1 t. balsamic vinegar
1 sweet onion, thinly sliced
8 thinly sliced slices sourdough bread
¼ c. jarred olive tapenade
1 red pepper, sliced into rings
1 green pepper, sliced into rings
1 yellow pepper, sliced into rings
1 c. spinach leaves
2 roma tomatoes, sliced
4 slices provolone cheese

Combine zucchini, squash and mushrooms in a large bowl; toss with one teaspoon olive oil and vinegar. Grill, covered, over medium-high heat (350 to 400 degrees) 15 to 20 minutes, turning occasionally; set aside. Heat one teaspoon olive oil in a skillet over medium heat. Add onion and cook 15 minutes or until caramelized, stirring often; set aside. Spread tops and bottoms of bread slices with tapénade; layer red pepper rings and next 5 ingredients evenly on half the bread slices and top with remaining bread slices. Preheat panini press according to manufacturer's instructions. Place sandwiches in press (in batches, if necessary); cook 3 to 4 minutes until cheese melts and bread is toasted.

Nutrition Per Serving: 395 calories, 12g fat, 6g sat fat, 19mg cholesterol, 673mg sodium, 55g carbohydrate, 6g fiber, 11g sugars, 19g protein.

Beverly Mock, *Pensacola, FL*

Turkey Fruit Salad

Host a summertime luncheon with girlfriends, then serve this delicious salad.

Serves 4

3 c. cooked turkey, cubed
¾ c. celery, chopped
1 c. seedless red grapes, halved
⅓ c. fresh pineapple, cubed
11-oz. can mandarin oranges, drained
¼ c. chopped pecans
¼ c. light mayonnaise-type salad dressing
⅛ t. salt
Garnish: lettuce leaves

Combine turkey, celery, grapes, pineapple, oranges and pecans together. Blend in salad dressing; sprinkle with salt. Chill until serving time. When ready to serve, spoon individual servings onto lettuce leaves.

Nutrition Per Serving: 295 calories, 11g fat, 2g sat fat, 85mg cholesterol, 262mg sodium, 16g carbohydrate, 2g fiber, 13g sugars, 33g protein.

Turkey Fruit Salad

Aubrey Dufour, *Salem, IN*

Tomato Garbanzo Salad

Try this tasty salad the next time you're looking for something new.

Makes 6 servings

1 c. elbow macaroni, uncooked
15-oz. can garbanzo beans, drained and rinsed
2 c. tomatoes, diced
1 c. celery, diced
1/2 c. red onion, diced
1/3 c. olive oil
1/4 c. lemon juice
2 T. fresh parsley, chopped
2 t. ground cumin
1/4 t. salt
1/2 t. pepper

Cook macaroni according to package directions; drain and rinse in cold water. Transfer to a large bowl and combine with remaining ingredients. Stir to mix well. Cover and chill at least one hour.

Nutrition Per Serving: 293 calories, 14g fat, 2g sat fat, 0mg cholesterol, 273mg sodium, 34g carbohydrate, 6g fiber, 6g sugars, 8g protein.

Lane McCloud, *Siloam Springs, AR*

Apple-Yogurt Coleslaw

The tart flavor of the apples, sweetness of the pineapple and cranberries and the crunch of the nuts add a fresh twist to coleslaw.

Makes 10 servings

1 c. plain non-fat yogurt
1/4 c. light mayonnaise
8-oz. can crushed pineapple
4 Granny Smith apples, cored and chopped
1/2 head purple cabbage, shredded
1/2 head green cabbage, shredded
1/4 c. red onion, finely chopped
1 carrot, peeled and shredded
1 stalk celery, diced
1/4 c. sugar
1/2 t. salt
1/4 t. pepper
1 t. mustard
3/4 c. sweetened dried cranberries
3/4 c. chopped walnuts
Garnish: cabbage leaves

Mix together yogurt, mayonnaise and pineapple with juice in a large bowl. Stir apples into yogurt mixture, coating well. Add remaining ingredients except cranberries, walnuts and garnish; mix well. Cover and chill for at least one hour. Before serving, stir in cranberries and walnuts. Serve on whole cabbage leaves.

Nutrition Per Serving: 217 calories, 8g fat, 1g sat fat, 2mg cholesterol, 223mg sodium, 36g carbohydrate, 6g fiber, 26g sugars, 4g protein.

Linda Karner, *Pisgah Forest, NC*

Wheat Berry & Wild Rice Salad

This is a recipe I created myself, and my family loves it! You can add any fresh herbs that you like. Be sure to allow enough time for the wheat berries to soak.

Makes 10 servings

3/4 c. wheat berries, uncooked
1 c. wild rice, uncooked
1 red or green pepper, diced
1 red onion, chopped
1/3 c. walnuts, toasted and coarsely chopped
1/4 c. fresh oregano, chopped
4 to 5 leaves fresh basil, chopped
3 sprigs fresh parsley, chopped
Vinaigrette Salad Dressing

Cover wheat berries with water in a saucepan; cover with lid and soak 8 hours to overnight. Drain wheat berries well; add fresh cold water to cover. Cook over medium heat one hour, or until tender; drain well. Meanwhile, in a separate saucepan, cover rice with cold water. Cook over medium heat 30 minutes, or until tender; drain well. Combine wheat berries and rice in a serving bowl. Stir in remaining ingredients. Toss with Vinaigrette Salad Dressing. For the best flavor, serve at room temperature; salad may also be served chilled.

VINAIGRETTE SALAD DRESSING:

3 T. lemon juice
1 T. canola oil
1 T. sugar

Whisk all ingredients together.

Nutrition Per Serving: 149 calories, 4g fat, 0g sat fat, 0mg cholesterol, 3mg sodium, 24g carbohydrate, 2g fiber, 3g sugars, 5g protein.

Wheat Berry & Wild Rice Salad

Joanna Nicoline-Haughey, *Berwyn, PA*

Tomato-Mozzarella Salad

I remember Mom serving this simple salad in the summertime, made with just-picked ingredients.

Serves 4

4 tomatoes, cubed
1 cucumber, sliced
1 c. fresh mozzarella cheese, cubed
1 T. fresh basil, chopped
3 T. extra-virgin olive oil
salt and pepper to taste

Mix tomatoes, cucumber, cheese and basil in a serving bowl. Drizzle with oil and toss to mix; sprinkle with salt and pepper.

Nutrition Per Serving: 223 calories, 17g fat, 4g sat fat, 18mg cholesterol, 223mg sodium, 9g carbohydrate, 2g fiber, 5g sugars, 10g protein.

Tiffany Brinkley, *Broomfield, CO*

Town Square Favorite

A visit with friends for the weekend took us to a farmers' market on the town square. We filled our baskets with veggies, herbs, even cheese! That same day, we made these yummy open-faced sandwiches for dinner.

Serves 4

3 T. butter
1½ c. sliced mushrooms
½ c. red onion, sliced and separated into rings
2 zucchini, thinly sliced
1 t. dried basil
½ t. garlic, finely chopped
¼ t. salt
¼ t. pepper
4 whole-wheat bagel thins, split
1 c. shredded Monterey Jack cheese, divided
2 tomatoes, sliced

Melt butter in a skillet over medium heat. Stir in all ingredients except bagels, cheese and tomatoes. Cook, stirring occasionally, until vegetables are crisp-tender, about 4 to 5 minutes. Arrange bagels on an ungreased baking sheet. Sprinkle one tablespoon cheese over each bagel half. Bake at 375 degrees for 5 minutes, or until cheese is melted. Remove from oven; top each with one slice tomato. Spoon on vegetable mixture; top with remaining cheese. Continue baking 4 to 5 minutes longer, until cheese is melted. Serve open-faced.

Nutrition Per Serving: 168 calories, 9g fat, 6g sat fat, 26mg cholesterol, 272mg sodium, 15g carbohydrate, 2g fiber, 3g sugars, 7g protein.

Town Square Favorite

Judy Manning, *Great Bend, KS*

Summer Spinach Salad

This salad is always made at our home with the first crop of homegrown spinach and green onions.

Serves 6

1 lb. spinach, torn
3 eggs, hard-boiled, peeled and sliced
6 slices bacon, crisply cooked and crumbled
6 green onions, thinly sliced

Arrange all ingredients in a salad bowl. Cover and refrigerate for about 2 hours. At serving time, shake Cider Vinegar Dressing and drizzle over salad. Toss until spinach is well coated; serve at once.

CIDER VINEGAR DRESSING:

¼ c. light olive oil
¼ c. cider vinegar
1 t. salt
⅛ t. pepper
1 clove garlic, quartered

Combine all ingredients in a jar with a tight-fitting lid; shake vigorously. Refrigerate. At serving time, remove garlic and discard.

Nutrition Per Serving: 197 calories, 16g fat, 3g sat fat, 105mg cholesterol, 681mg sodium, 5g carbohydrate, 2g fiber, 1g sugars, 10g protein.

Lydia McCormick, *Burkburnett, TX*

Seaside Salmon Buns

Using canned salmon makes these yummy sandwiches super quick & easy!

Serves 6

14-oz. can salmon, drained and flaked
¼ c. green pepper, chopped
1 T. onion, chopped
2 t. lemon juice
½ c. low-fat mayonnaise
6 pretzel buns, split
½ c. low-fat shredded Cheddar cheese

Mix salmon, pepper, onion, lemon juice and mayonnaise. Pile salmon mixture onto bottom bun halves; sprinkle with cheese. Arrange salmon-topped buns on an ungreased baking sheet. Broil until lightly golden and cheese is melted. Top with remaining bun halves.

Nutrition Per Serving: 302 calories, 12g fat, 3g sat fat, 78mg cholesterol, 662mg sodium, 26g carbohydrate, 1g fiber, 1g sugars, 23g protein.

Seaside Salmon Buns

Chapter Three

Time for a Snack

Get ready for some quick-to-make **Appetizers, Smoothies and Beverages** that are as good for you as they are yummy! Try your hand at making easy-to-grab Mini Ham & Swiss Frittatas for a simple snack. A fresh and pretty Cranberry Slush is a cool, welcoming drink for a hot summer afternoon. Baja Shrimp Quesadillas will be the life of the party! So when you need a nibble or just something to tide you over to the next meal, choose a homemade bite of healthy goodness.

Checkerboard Cheese Sandwiches

Vickie, *Gooseberry Patch*

Checkerboard Cheese Sandwiches

These dainty little sandwiches are always a must-have at our card club parties. Stack the sliced bread when you cut off the crusts and it will take less time.

Makes 40, serves 20

2 c. low-fat shredded extra-sharp
   Cheddar cheese
2 c. shredded Swiss cheese
1 c. light mayonnaise
4-oz. jar diced pimentos, drained
1 t. dried, minced onion
¼ t. pepper
20 thin slices white bread, crusts trimmed
20 thin slices wheat bread, crusts trimmed

Stir together first 6 ingredients. Spread half of mixture on 10 white bread slices; top with remaining half of white bread slices. Spread remaining mixture on 10 wheat bread slices; top with remaining half of wheat bread slices. Cut each sandwich into 4 squares. Arrange, stacked in pairs, in a pattern, alternating white and wheat.

Nutrition Per Serving: 239 calories, 10g fat, 4g sat fat, 18mg cholesterol, 446mg sodium, 26g carbohydrate, 3g fiber, 4g sugars, 12g protein.

Betty Reeves, *Cardington, OH*

Stuffed Cherry Tomatoes

These little appetizers are a real hit at family picnics, especially with homegrown cherry tomatoes just ripened and picked off the vine.

Makes 24, serves 12

6 slices bacon, crisply cooked and crumbled
24 cherry tomatoes
½ c. light mayonnaise
½ c. green onion, finely chopped
2 T. fresh parsley, chopped
salt and pepper to taste

Set aside prepared bacon on paper towels to drain. Cut a thin slice off the top of each cherry tomato; discard slices. Use a small spoon to hollow out tomatoes; discard pulp. Combine remaining ingredients in a bowl; blend well. Spoon mixture into hollowed-out tomatoes. Refrigerate until chilled.

Nutrition Per Serving: 58 calories, 4g fat, 1g sat fat, 7mg cholesterol, 182mg sodium, 3g carbohydrate, 1g fiber, 1g sugars, 2g protein.

Happy Presentation

─────────── ✳ ───────────

Serve stuffed cherry tomatoes on a round plate, placing the tomatoes around the edge. Add fresh veggies in the middle.

Cindy Brown, *Farmington Hills, MI*

Country Herb Spread

For variety, omit chives and dill; add one teaspoon fresh oregano and ½ teaspoon each fresh thyme, basil and marjoram. Serve with your favorite crackers.

Makes 1 ½ cups, serves 12

8-oz. pkg. light cream cheese, softened
1 T. mayonnaise
1 t. Dijon mustard
1 T. fresh chives, chopped
1 T. fresh dill, chopped
1 clove garlic, pressed

Combine all ingredients except crackers; stir until well blended. Chill.

Nutrition Per Serving: 47 calories, 4g fat, 2g sat fat, 11mg cholesterol, 100mg sodium, 2g carbohydrate, 0g fiber, 1g sugars, 2g protein.

Charlotte Page, *Jay, ME*

Spring Tonic

A sweet-tart drink that's oh-so refreshing when spring comes around. I serve it on our deck when friends come over.

Makes 3 to 4 quarts, serves 8

2 lbs. rhubarb, chopped
4 c. water
¾ c. sugar
ice

Combine rhubarb and water in a saucepan; simmer over medium-low heat until rhubarb is soft. Strain and discard rhubarb, reserving liquid. Pour into a large pitcher; add sugar to taste. Chill until ready to serve. Serve in tall glasses over ice.

Nutrition Per Serving: 96 calories, 0g fat, 0g sat fat, 0mg cholesterol, 9mg sodium, 24g carbohydrate, 2g fiber, 20g sugars, 1g protein.

Jo Ann, *Gooseberry Patch*

Apple & Brie Toasts

These little tidbits of flavor are so showy and easy to make. We make them often!

Makes 2 ½ dozen, serves 30

1 baguette, cut into ¼-inch-thick slices
¼ c. brown sugar, packed
¼ c. chopped walnuts
3 T. butter, melted
13.2-oz. pkg. Brie cheese, thinly sliced
3 Granny Smith apples and/or Braeburn
    apples, cored and sliced

Arrange baguette slices on an ungreased baking sheet; bake at 350 degrees until lightly toasted. Set aside. Mix together brown sugar, walnuts and butter. Top each slice of bread with a cheese slice, an apple slice and ½ teaspoon of brown sugar mixture. Bake at 350 degrees until cheese melts, 2 to 4 minutes.

Nutrition Per Serving: 91 calories, 5g fat, 3g sat fat, 16mg cholesterol, 110mg sodium, 7g carbohydrate, 1g fiber, 4g sugars, 3g protein.

Apple & Brie Toasts

Shirl Parsons, *Cape Carteret, NC*

Creamy Raspberry Smoothie

Cool and refreshing, this smoothie delivers a double dose of raspberry flavor with the addition of fresh raspberries and raspberry sherbet. Garnish with a sprig of mint, and you've got a sweet smoothie pretty enough for company.

Makes 3 ½ cups, serves 4

1¾ c. fresh raspberries, frozen
1¼ c. white grape juice
1½ c. raspberry sherbet
1 T. lemon juice
Optional: fresh mint sprigs

Place raspberries and grape juice in a blender and process until smooth; strain mixture and return to blender. Add sherbet and lemon juice; cover and process until smooth. Garnish with fresh mint, if desired. Serve immediately.

Nutrition Per Serving: 158 calories, 1g fat, 1g sat fat, 1mg cholesterol, 32mg sodium, 36g carbohydrate, 4g fiber, 28g sugars, 1g protein.

Debi DeVore, *Dover, OH*

Spiced Orange Pecans

A tasty hostess gift that's sure to be welcome.

Makes about 3 ½ cups, serves 16

2 egg whites, beaten
3 T. orange juice
2 c. pecan halves
1 c. powdered sugar
2 T. cornstarch
1 T. orange zest
1 t. cinnamon
¾ t. ground cloves
¼ t. allspice
⅛ t. salt

Combine egg whites and orange juice. Add pecans and toss to coat; drain. In a separate bowl, combine remaining ingredients. Add pecans and toss to coat. Spread in a single layer in a greased 15"x10" jelly-roll pan. Bake at 250 degrees for 30 to 35 minutes, until dry and lightly golden. Cool completely; store in airtight container.

Nutrition Per Serving: 123 calories, 9g fat, 1g sat fat, 0mg cholesterol, 26mg sodium, 11g carbohydrate, 1g fiber, 8g sugars, 2g protein.

Spiced Orange Pecans

Kelly Wilkie, *Garnet Valley, PA*

Yummy Spinach Balls

These savory warm spinach bites are always a hit at parties.

Makes 20 servings

10-oz. pkg. frozen chopped spinach, thawed
   and drained
6-oz. pkg. herb-flavored stuffing mix
5 eggs, beaten
1 onion, chopped
½ c. butter, melted
½ t. pepper
¼ t. garlic powder
¼ t. dried thyme

In a bowl, mix all ingredients well. Form into one to 1½-inch balls. Place on an ungreased baking sheet; freeze for at least 30 minutes, until firm. Remove from freezer and place on well-greased baking sheets. Bake, uncovered, at 375 degrees for 25 minutes, or until lightly golden. Spinach balls may be stored in freezer in plastic freezer bags up to one month; bake at serving time.

Nutrition Per Serving: 98 calories, 6g fat, 3g sat fat, 59mg cholesterol, 149mg sodium, 8g carbohydrate, 1g fiber, 1g sugars, 3g protein.

Kathy Wood, *La Crescenta, CA*

Oven-Baked Chicken Fingers

Heating your baking sheet prior to cooking ensures crispier results for your chicken fingers. Serve them with ranch dressing, barbecue sauce or honey mustard for dipping.

Serves 12

1 c. Italian-flavored dry bread crumbs
2 T. grated Parmesan cheese
1 clove garlic, minced
¼ c. oil
6 boneless, skinless chicken breasts

Preheat oven to 425 degrees. Heat a baking sheet in the oven for 5 minutes. Combine bread crumbs and cheese in a shallow dish; set aside. Combine garlic and oil in a small bowl; set aside. Place chicken between 2 sheets of heavy-duty plastic wrap. Flatten chicken to ½-inch thickness, using a meat mallet or rolling pin; cut into one-inch-wide strips. Dip strips in oil mixture; coat with crumb mixture. Coat preheated baking sheet with non-stick vegetable spray and place chicken on prepared baking sheet. Bake at 425 degrees for 12 to 14 minutes, turning after 10 minutes.

Nutrition Per Serving: 225 calories, 8g fat, 2g sat fat, 87mg cholesterol, 245mg sodium, 7g carbohydrate, 0g fiber, 1g sugars, 28g protein.

Oven-Baked Chicken Fingers

Marianne's Cranberry Roll-Ups

Sandi Giverson, *Vero Beach, FL*

Marianne's Cranberry Roll-Ups

One of the girls I work with, Marianne Hudgins, always has the best recipes! With her permission, here is one of my favorites.

Serves 10

8-oz. container light whipped cream cheese
8-oz. pkg. crumbled feta cheese
6-oz. pkg. dried cranberries
3 T. chives, chopped
4 10-inch whole-grain flour tortillas

Combine all ingredients except tortillas together; blend until smooth. Spread mixture over tortillas, roll up and wrap in plastic wrap; chill until ready to serve. Cut each roll into one-inch slices.

Nutrition Per Serving: 218 calories, 10g fat, 6g sat fat, 32mg cholesterol, 507mg sodium, 25g carbohydrate, 1g fiber, 9g sugars, 7g protein.

Susie Backus, *Delaware, OH*

Sweet & Saucy Spareribs

These scrumptious ribs are equally at home at a summer picnic or at a lucky New Year's Day dinner.

Makes 8 servings

2 lbs. pork spareribs, sliced into serving-size portions
10¾-oz. can tomato soup
1 onion, chopped
3 cloves garlic, minced
1 T. brown sugar, packed
1 T. Worcestershire sauce
2 T. low-sodium soy sauce
¼ c. cold water
1 t. cornstarch

Place ribs in a stockpot and add water to cover. Bring to a boil; reduce heat and simmer for 15 minutes. Drain; arrange ribs in a slow cooker. Mix together remaining ingredients except cold water and cornstarch; pour over ribs. Cover and cook on low setting for 6 to 8 hours. When ribs are tender, place them on a serving platter; cover to keep warm. Pour sauce from slow cooker into a saucepan over medium-high heat. Stir together cold water and cornstarch; stir into sauce and bring to a boil. Cook and stir until sauce has reached desired thickness. Serve ribs with sauce.

Nutrition Per Serving: 350 calories, 27g fat, 9g sat fat, 91mg cholesterol, 370mg sodium, 8g carbohydrate, 1g fiber, 5g sugars, 18g protein.

Happy Presentation
··········· ✳ ···········
Stack small plates beside the serving platter and add a basket of colorful napkins rolled and tied with twine.

Lisa Johnson, *Hallsville, TX*

Crispy Potato Fingers

My mama always made these "tater fingers" for my kids when they would come see her for a visit. The kids are both grown now, and they still love it when Granny makes these yummy potatoes!

Makes 4 servings

3 c. corn flake cereal
3 T. grated Parmesan cheese
1 t. paprika
¼ t. garlic salt
3 T. butter, melted
2 baking potatoes, peeled and cut into strips

Place cereal, cheese and seasonings into a blender or food processor. Process until crushed and well mixed. Pour cereal mixture into a pie plate or shallow dish; place melted butter in a separate shallow dish. Dip potato strips into butter, then into cereal mixture, coating well. Arrange potato strips on a greased baking sheet. Bake at 375 degrees for 25 minutes, or until tender and golden.

Nutrition Per Serving: 214 calories, 10g fat, 6g sat fat, 27mg cholesterol, 359mg sodium, 27g carbohydrate, 2g fiber, 2g sugars, 4g protein.

Judy Borecky, *Escondido, CA*

Cranberry Slush

Create a festive garnish for each glass...just slip the cranberries and orange and lime slices onto wooden skewers.

Makes 23 ½ cups, serves 20

¾ c. sugar
8 c. water, divided
2 c. white grape juice
12-oz. can frozen orange juice concentrate
12-oz. can frozen cranberry juice cocktail concentrate
6-oz. can frozen limeade concentrate
2-ltr. bottle lemon-lime soda, chilled
Garnishes: fresh cranberries, orange slices, lime slices

Combine sugar and 2 cups water in a large saucepan over medium heat, stirring until sugar dissolves. Add grape juice, frozen fruit concentrates and remaining 6 cups water. Pour into 2 one-gallon-size heavy-duty plastic zipping bags; freeze until solid. To serve, place frozen mixture into a punch bowl; pour chilled lemon-lime soda over mixture. Stir to break up chunks until mixture is slushy. Garnish each individual serving, if desired.

Nutrition Per Serving: 191 calories, 0g fat, 0g sat fat, 0mg cholesterol, 17mg sodium, 48g carbohydrate, 0g fiber, 44g sugars, 1g protein.

Cranberry Slush

Place wings in a large plastic zipping bag; set aside. Combine soy sauce and next 5 ingredients; pour over wings, turning to coat. Refrigerate overnight, turning several times. Drain wings, discarding marinade; arrange in a single layer on an ungreased jelly-roll pan. Bake at 450 degrees for 25 to 30 minutes, until golden and juices run clear when chicken is pierced with a fork. Serve with celery and ranch dressing, if desired.

Nutrition Per Serving: 146 calories, 4g fat, 1g sat fat, 65mg cholesterol, 136mg sodium, 1g carbohydrate, 0g fiber, 1g sugars, 25g protein.

Susanne Erickson, *Columbus, OH*

Chinese Chicken Wings

Move over, hot wings. These Asian-inspired chicken wings are packed with flavor and they're baked. Make extra, because the crowd will love them!

Makes 2 to 3 dozen, serves 12

3 lbs. chicken wings
½ c. low-sodium soy sauce
1 c. pineapple juice
⅓ c. brown sugar, packed
1 t. ground ginger
1 t. garlic salt
½ t. pepper
Optional: celery sticks and ranch salad dressing

Jill Ball, *Highland, UT*

Sweet & Tangy Fruit Dip

As a mother, I'm always looking for easy, healthy snack ideas, so I created this recipe.

Makes 10 servings

1 c. low-fat cottage cheese
3 T. low-fat plain yogurt
2 t. honey
1 T. orange juice
2½ T. orange marmalade
2 T. unsweetened flaked coconut
favorite fresh fruit, sliced

Place all ingredients except coconut and fruit in a food processor. Process until smooth and creamy. Stir in coconut. Refrigerate until chilled. Serve with a variety of fresh fruit.

Nutrition Per Serving: 41 calories, 1g fat, 0g sat fat, 1mg cholesterol, 100mg sodium, 6g carbohydrate, 0g fiber, 6g sugars, 3g protein.

Sweet & Tangy Fruit Dip

Lynda's Spinach-Feta Dip

Lynda McCormick, *Burkburnett, TX*

Lynda's Spinach-Feta Dip

This is a favorite dip enjoyed with bread cubes or crackers. Try garnishing with some farm-fresh chopped tomatoes too.

Makes 2 cups, serves 8

8-oz. container Greek yogurt
¾ c. crumbled low-fat feta cheese
¼ c. light cream cheese, softened
¼ c. light sour cream
1 clove garlic, pressed
1½ c. baby spinach, finely chopped
1 T. fresh dill, minced, or 1 t. dill weed
⅛ t. pepper
Optional: additional minced fresh dill
pita or bagel chips

Combine yogurt, cheeses, sour cream and garlic in a food processor. Process until smooth, scraping sides once. Spoon yogurt mixture into a bowl; stir in spinach, dill and pepper. Cover and refrigerate for several hours, until chilled. Let stand for 10 minutes at room temperature before serving. If desired, garnish with additional dill; serve with chips.

Nutrition Per Serving: 82 calories, 5g fat, 3g sat fat, 21mg cholesterol, 184mg sodium, 3g carbohydrate, 0g fiber, 2g sugars, 6g protein.

Christine Gabriel, *Hay Market, PA*

Teriyaki Chicken Skewers

The little bit of apricot jam and ground ginger in the sauce makes these chicken bites extra good!

Serves 6

¼ c. low-sodium soy sauce
¼ c. brown sugar, packed
2 t. apricot jam
½ t. ground ginger
2 cloves garlic, pressed
2 boneless, skinless chicken breasts, cut into
    1-inch cubes
8 green onions, cut into 1-inch lengths
6 8-inch skewers, soaked in water

Whisk together soy sauce, brown sugar, jam, ginger and garlic in a shallow bowl. Add chicken to sauce; toss to coat. Cover and refrigerate for one to 8 hours, stirring occasionally. Alternate chicken and onions on skewers, reserving marinade. Broil for 10 minutes, or until chicken is cooked through, turning several times and basting with reserved marinade. Discard any of the remaining marinade.

Nutrition Per Serving: 225 calories, 3g fat, 1g sat fat, 88mg cholesterol, 439mg sodium, 13g carbohydrate, 1g fiber, 11g sugars, 36g protein.

Judy Bailey, *Des Moines, IA*

Strawberry Preserves Smoothies

We love to make these smoothies for a quick snack or even for a drink at dinnertime. We like strawberries so much that we choose that flavor, but you can use raspberries or any other fruit you like.

Makes 4 servings

2 T. strawberry preserves
1 c. crushed pineapple
1 c. orange juice
3 c. fresh strawberries, hulled and sliced
8-oz. container low-fat strawberry yogurt
8-oz. container low-fat plain yogurt

Combine all ingredients in a blender; process until smooth. Pour into chilled jelly jars to serve.

Nutrition Per Serving: 227 calories, 2g fat, 1g sat fat, 7mg cholesterol, 79mg sodium, 47g carbohydrate, 3g fiber, 30g sugars, 7g protein.

⁓ Healthy Fact ⁓

Strawberries have so many wonderful qualities... they are pretty, tasty and readily available. They are also a good source of vitamin C, manganese, folate and potassium.

Ashley Connelly, *Louisa, VA*

Fruit Salsa with Cinnamon Chips

Kiwis, apples, raspberries and strawberries make up this colorful salsa. It'll be a treat that guests will not want to miss...especially when served with your homemade cinnamon-favored chips.

Serves 15

2 kiwi, peeled and diced
2 Golden Delicious apples, peeled. cored and diced
½ lb. raspberries
16-oz. pkg. strawberries, hulled and diced
1 c. plus 2 T. sugar, divided
1 T. brown sugar, packed
3 T. strawberry preserves
1 to 2 T. cinnamon
10 10-inch flour tortillas, sliced into wedges
butter-flavored non-stick vegetable spray

Combine all prepared fruit in a large bowl; mix in 2 tablespoons sugar, brown sugar and strawberry preserves. Cover and chill at least 15 minutes. Mix together remaining sugar and cinnamon; set aside. Arrange tortilla wedges in a single layer on an ungreased baking sheet; coat chips with butter-flavored vegetable spray. Sprinkle with desired amount of cinnamon-sugar. Bake at 350 degrees for 8 to 10 minutes. Repeat with remaining tortilla wedges; cool 15 minutes. Serve chips with chilled fruit mixture.

Nutrition Per Serving: 248 calories, 3g fat, 1g sat fat, 0mg cholesterol, 323mg sodium, 51g carbohydrate, 3g fiber, 25g sugars, 4g protein.

Fruit Salsa with Cinnamon Chips

Oh-So-Fruity Lemonade

Jamie Johnson, *Hilliard, OH*

Oh-So-Fruity Lemonade

When it's time to cool off on a summer day, a tall glass of this fruity lemonade will do the trick!

Makes 2 quarts, serves 4

12-oz. can frozen lemonade concentrate, thawed
2 c. cold water
1½ c. mango juice
½ c. red or green grapes, halved
½ c. pineapple, chopped
½ c. mango, peeled, pitted and chopped
½ c. strawberries, hulled and chopped
½ c. raspberries
ice

Combine lemonade concentrate, water and juice in a large pitcher. Stir in fruit. Serve immediately over ice, or cover and chill up to one hour.

Nutrition Per Serving: 307 calories, 1g fat, 0g sat fat, 0mg cholesterol, 18mg sodium, 75g carbohydrate, 3g fiber, 69g sugars, 1g protein.

Marion Sundberg, *Ramona, CA*

Blue Cheese Spread

While on vacation, we stopped at a wonderful California winery to taste the wine. They had something similar to this yummy spread to eat while tasting their sparkling wine.

Serves 12

8-oz. pkg. light cream cheese, softened
4-oz. pkg. crumbled blue cheese
½ c. dry sparkling white wine or sparkling white grape juice
cracked pepper to taste
½ c. chopped pecans
¼ c. fresh chives, snipped

Combine cream cheese and blue cheese. Stir in wine or grape juice until desired consistency is reached. Add remaining ingredients except crackers; blend well. Serve with crackers.

Nutrition Per Serving: 111 calories, 9g fat, 4g sat fat, 17mg cholesterol, 197mg sodium, 3g carbohydrate, 0g fiber, 1g sugars, 4g protein.

Marian Smith, *Columbus, OH*

Fiesta Guacamole

This was a tasty and welcome addition to our office Fiesta Party!

Makes 10 servings

4 avocados, peeled, pitted, cubed and mashed
2 tomatoes, diced
½ onion, diced
1 bunch fresh cilantro, chopped
1 jalapeño pepper, chopped
1 T. garlic, minced
juice of 2 limes

Blend together avocados and tomatoes. Stir in onion, cilantro, jalapeño and garlic. Add lime juice; mix well. Cover and refrigerate for 45 minutes before serving.

Nutrition Per Serving: 101 calories, 8g fat, 1g sat fat, 0mg cholesterol, 7mg sodium, 7g carbohydrate, 4g fiber, 1g sugars, 1g protein.

Pecan-Stuffed Deviled Eggs

Jo Ann, *Gooseberry Patch*

Pecan-Stuffed Deviled Eggs

Make these deviled eggs fun and festive by adding snipped parsley and chopped pecans as a garnish.

Serves 6

6 eggs, hard-boiled and peeled
¼ c. mayonnaise
1 t. onion, grated
½ t. fresh parsley, chopped
½ t. dry mustard
⅛ t. salt
⅓ c. pecans, coarsely chopped
Garnish: fresh parsley, chopped pecans

Cut eggs in half lengthwise and carefully remove yolks. Mash yolks in a small bowl. Stir in mayonnaise and next 4 ingredients; blend well. Stir in pecans. Spoon or pipe yolk mixture evenly into egg-white halves. Garnish, if desired.

Nutrition Per Serving: 180 calories, 16g fat, 3g sat fat, 193mg cholesterol, 173mg sodium, 1g carbohydrate, 1g fiber, 0g sugars, 7g protein.

Evelyn Thorpe, *Lodi, CA*

Energy Boost Smoothies

I'm not a coffee drinker, so this smoothie gives me the boost of energy that I need first thing in the morning. I vary the kind of berries I use, but I always use the carrot and spinach to get enough veggies.

Makes 2 servings

1 ripe banana, sliced
5 strawberries, hulled
⅓ c. fresh or frozen blueberries
1 carrot, peeled and sliced
1 apple, cored and quartered
1 orange, peeled and sectioned
½ c. baby spinach
1 c. ice cubes
½ c. water
Optional: flax seed to taste

Combine all ingredients in a food processor or blender. Process until smooth and well mixed; pour into tall glasses.

Nutrition Per Serving: 207 calories, 1g fat, 0g sat fat, 0mg cholesterol, 42mg sodium, 50g carbohydrate, 10g fiber, 23g sugars, 3g protein.

Kitchen Helper

Whip up deviled eggs in no time by combining ingredients in a plastic zipping bag instead of a bowl. Blend by squeezing the bag, then snip off a corner and pipe the filling into the egg white halves.

Connie Bryant, *Topeka, KS*

Easy Meatballs in Sauce

These make great little appetizers or spoon these yummy meatballs into crusty hard rolls or serve over pasta. Pass the Parmesan cheese, please!

Makes 8 servings

1½ lbs. ground beef
1¼ c. Italian-seasoned dry bread crumbs
¼ c. fresh parsley, chopped
2 cloves garlic, minced
1 onion, chopped
1 egg, beaten
28-oz. jar spaghetti sauce
16-oz. can crushed tomatoes
14¼-oz. can tomato purée

In a large bowl, combine all ingredients except spaghetti sauce, tomatoes and tomato purée. Mix by hand and form into 16 meatballs; set aside. In a slow cooker, stir together remaining ingredients. Add meatballs to sauce mixture and turn to coat. Cover and cook on low setting for 6 to 8 hours.

Nutrition Per Serving: 330 calories, 12g fat, 4g sat fat, 79mg cholesterol, 944mg sodium, 33g carbohydrate, 6g fiber, 12g sugars, 24g protein.

Louise McGaha, *Clinton, TN*

Traditional Hummus

I love this recipe...it's just right for a snack or a quick appetizer.

Makes 2 cups, serves 10

2 15-oz. cans garbanzo beans, drained and rinsed
½ c. warm water
3 T. lime or lemon juice
1 T. tahini sesame seed paste
1½ t. ground cumin
1 T. garlic, minced
¼ t. salt

Place all ingredients in a food processor or blender. Process until mixture is very smooth, about 4 minutes. If a thinner consistency is desired, add an extra tablespoon or 2 of water. Transfer to a serving bowl.

Nutrition Per Serving: 129 calories, 3g fat, 0g sat fat, 0mg cholesterol, 242mg sodium, 21g carbohydrate, 6g fiber, 4g sugars, 6g protein.

> ~ **Healthy Fact** ~
>
> Garbanzo beans (also called chickpeas) have long been valued for their fiber content. They are also very filling and oh-so-delicious!

Traditional Hummus

thoroughly and keep warm over low heat. If desired, serve topped with marshmallows or whipped topping and peppermint sticks.

Nutrition Per Serving: 114 calories, 2g fat, 1g sat fat, 7mg cholesterol, 123mg sodium, 20g carbohydrate, 1g fiber, 17g sugars, 4g protein.

Lisa Allbright, *Crockett, TX*

Hot Chocolate Supreme

Curl up and enjoy a mug of this chocolatey cocoa on a frosty winter's day.

Makes 8 ¾ cups, serves 8

½ c. sugar
½ c. baking cocoa
¼ t. salt
5 c. water
3 c. 2% milk
Optional: marshmallows, whipped topping, peppermint sticks

Combine sugar, cocoa and salt in a saucepan; whisk in water. Bring to a boil over high heat, stirring until sugar is completely dissolved. Reduce heat to medium; add milk. Heat

Regina Vining, *Warwick, RI*

Spiced Chocolate Coffee

Adding the spices to this coffee drink makes it seem like it came from an expensive coffee house! Add a little milk to the mixture if you like a creamy drink.

Serves 8

8 c. brewed coffee
2 T. sugar
¼ c. chocolate syrup
4 4-inch cinnamon sticks
1½ t. whole cloves

Combine first 3 ingredients in a large stockpot. Wrap spices in a coffee filter and tie with kitchen string; add to pot. Cover and simmer for 20 minutes. Remove and discard spices. Ladle coffee into mugs.

Nutrition Per Serving: 41 calories, 0g fat, 0g sat fat, 0mg cholesterol, 12mg sodium, 9g carbohydrate, 0g fiber, 8g sugars, 0g protein.

Cynde Sonnier, *Mont Belvieu, TX*

Pineapple-Pecan Cheese Spread

This is a delicious, fast-fix recipe and always yummy with fresh veggies or pieces of toasted whole-grain bread. The combination of the sweet crushed pineapple and the spicy chiles and red peppers is just perfect!

Serves 8

2 8-oz. pkgs. light cream cheese, softened
1½ c. reduced-fat shredded Cheddar cheese
¾ c. chopped pecans, toasted and divided
¾ c. crushed pineapple, drained
4-oz. can chopped green chiles, drained
2 T. roasted red peppers, chopped
½ t. garlic powder

In a large bowl, beat cream cheese until smooth. Add Cheddar cheese, ¾ cup pecans, pineapple, chiles, red pepper and garlic powder; beat until thoroughly combined. Transfer to a serving dish. Cover and refrigerate. When ready to serve, sprinkle with remaining pecans.

Nutrition Per Serving: 262 calories, 20g fat, 8g sat fat, 42mg cholesterol, 507mg sodium, 11g carbohydrate, 1g fiber, 7g sugars, 11g protein.

April Haury, *Paramus, NJ*

Mom's Best Fruit Smoothies

This simple smoothie is one of our family favorites...and so easy!

Makes 3 servings

1½ c. fresh or frozen peaches, cut into chunks
2 mangoes, pitted and diced
1 banana, cut into chunks
8-oz. container non-fat plain yogurt
1 T. honey

Combine fruit and yogurt in a blender. Process until smooth; pour into tall glasses.

Nutrition Per Serving: 205 calories, 1g fat, 0g sat fat, 3mg cholesterol, 53mg sodium, 48g carbohydrate, 4g fiber, 40g sugars, 6g protein.

Quick & Easy Summer Salsa

Chris Nelson, *New Berlin, WI*

Quick & Easy Summer Salsa

There is absolutely nothing like garden-fresh salsa. If you can't wait for it to chill, no problem...it's terrific enjoyed right away!

Makes 2½ to 3 cups, serves 6

10 roma tomatoes, chopped
1 c. fresh cilantro, chopped
½ c. red onion, chopped
1 T. vinegar
½ c. olive oil
juice of 2 key limes
tortilla chips

Combine all ingredients except chips in a bowl; stir to blend. Refrigerate until chilled. Serve with tortilla chips.

Nutrition Per Serving: 248 calories, 21g fat, 3g sat fat, 0mg cholesterol, 61mg sodium, 14g carbohydrate, 2g fiber, 4g sugars, 2g protein.

Kathy Harris, *Valley Center, KS*

Fast & Easy Red Pepper Hummus

I experimented with several recipes and came up with this quick, easy and delicious new one. Our friends just love it served with pita chips.

Serves 8

2 15-oz. cans chickpeas, drained and rinsed
2 T. taco seasoning mix
1 c. roasted red peppers, chopped
olive oil to taste

Purèe chickpeas, taco seasoning and roasted red peppers together in a food processor. Drizzle in olive oil until desired consistency is reached. Chill one hour before serving. Makes 2 cups.

Nutrition Per Serving: 171 calories, 5g fat, 1g sat fat, 0mg cholesterol, 283mg sodium, 26g carbohydrate, 7g fiber, 5g sugars, 8g protein.

Cheri Maxwell, *Gulf Breeze, FL*

Berry-Citrus Smoothies

A super-tasty, 3-ingredient recipe that's ready in a snap.

Makes 4 servings

1 pt. strawberries, hulled and sliced
1 c. plain low-fat yogurt
1 c. frozen lemon or orange sorbet

Combine all ingredients in a blender; process until smooth. Pour into glasses to serve.

Nutrition Per Serving: 118 calories, 2g fat, 1g sat fat, 4mg cholesterol, 61mg sodium, 22g carbohydrate, 2g fiber, 17g sugars, 4g protein.

Baja Shrimp Quesadillas

Jo Ann, *Gooseberry Patch*

Baja Shrimp Quesadillas

These quesadillas are always a special treat with all the yummy ingredients inside each tasty little serving. Everyone loves them!

Makes about 4 dozen, serves 48

2 ½ lbs. shrimp, peeled and cleaned
3 c. shredded Cheddar cheese
½ c. mayonnaise
¾ c. salsa
¼ t. ground cumin
¼ t. cayenne pepper
¼ t. pepper
12 6-inch flour tortillas
Garnish: plain Greek yogurt, chopped fresh
    parsley

Chop shrimp, discarding tails. Mix shrimp, cheese, mayonnaise, salsa, cumin and peppers; spread one to 2 tablespoons on one tortilla. Place another tortilla on top; put on a greased baking sheet. Repeat with remaining tortillas. Bake at 350 degrees for 15 minutes; remove and cut into small triangles. Garnish as desired.

Nutrition Per Serving: 89 calories, 5g fat, 2g sat fat, 46mg cholesterol, 165mg sodium, 4g carbohydrate, 0g fiber, 1g sugars, 7g protein.

Danyel Martin, *Madisonville, KY*

Crabmeat Dip

This recipe was given to me by my mom. It is wonderful to take to a potluck for work or a family gathering. I took this to a black-tie event with my husband's boss and it was the hit of the party.

Serves 20

8-oz. pkg. light cream cheese, softened
1 t. lemon juice
2 t. onion, minced
1½ T. crumbled blue cheese
12-oz. jar cocktail sauce
6-oz. can crabmeat, drained

Blend together cream cheese, lemon juice, minced onion and blue cheese. Spread evenly on a plate; spread with cocktail sauce to cover. Sprinkle with crabmeat. Serve with crackers.

Nutrition Per Serving: 55 calories, 2g fat, 1g sat fat, 14mg cholesterol, 258mg sodium, 6g carbohydrate, 0g fiber, 3g sugars, 3g protein.

Happy Presentation

⁕

A shallow pie plate works well to serve cream cheese dips. Choose one that has fluted edges or in a pretty color to match the theme of the party.

Barb Stout, *Delaware, OH*

Minty Orange Iced Tea

We love that this makes such a big batch of tea...we drink it up and make more!

Makes 8 servings

6 c. water
8 tea bags
¼ c. fresh mint, chopped
3 T. sugar
2 c. orange juice
juice of 2 lemons
ice

Bring water to a boil in a saucepan. Remove from heat and add tea bags, mint and sugar; steep for 5 minutes. Discard tea bags; strain out mint. Chill for at least 2 hours. Pour into a large pitcher; add juices. Serve in tall glasses over ice.

Nutrition Per Serving: 51 calories, 0g fat, 0g sat fat, 0mg cholesterol, 9mg sodium, 13g carbohydrate, 0g fiber, 10g sugars, 0g protein.

Kitchen Helper

Keep slices of lemon and lime in a sealed plastic container in your fridge for a touch of citrus in drinks and special dishes.

Charlotte Smith, *Tyrone, PA*

Tangy Meatballs

The chili sauce in these meatballs makes them extra good...a secret you can share with the ones that ask for the recipe!

Makes 4 dozen, serves 24

2 lbs. lean ground beef
2 eggs, beaten
½ t. salt
¾ c. quick-cooking oats, uncooked
1⅓ c. chili sauce, divided
¼ c. grape jelly
Optional: dried parsley

Combine ground beef, eggs, salt, oats and ⅓ cup chili sauce. Shape into one-inch balls; place in an ungreased shallow baking pan. Bake at 400 degrees for 15 to 17 minutes; drain. Combine grape jelly and remaining chili sauce in a large saucepan; cover and cook over medium heat, stirring occasionally until mixture is well blended. Add meatballs and continue cooking until heated through. Sprinkle with parsley, if desired.

Nutrition Per Serving: 107 calories, 4g fat, 2g sat fat, 40mg cholesterol, 284mg sodium, 7g carbohydrate, 1g fiber, 3g sugars, 9g protein.

Tangy Meatballs

Kristin Zurek, *Berkeley, CA*

Shrimp-Stuffed Tomato Poppers

If you have them or can find them, using heirloom cherry tomatoes in different colors makes these poppers extra pretty!

Serves 16

2 pts. cherry tomatoes
½ lb. cooked shrimp, peeled and finely
    chopped
8-oz. pkg. light cream cheese, softened
¼ c. light mayonnaise
¼ c. grated Parmesan cheese
1 t. prepared horseradish
1 t. lemon juice
salt and pepper to taste
Garnish: chopped fresh parsley

Cut a thin slice off the top of each tomato; scoop out and discard pulp. Place tomatoes upside-down on a paper towel; let drain for 30 minutes. Combine remaining ingredients except parsley; blend until smooth. Spoon into tomatoes; sprinkle with parsley.

Nutrition Per Serving: 63 calories, 4g fat, 2g sat fat, 32mg cholesterol, 142mg sodium, 3g carbohydrate, 0g fiber, 2g sugars, 5g protein.

Kathy Wood, *La Crescenta, CA*

Texas Caviar

This dip is a hands-down crowd pleaser. Serve it with your favorite multi-colored tortilla chips. Such a pretty appetizer!

Makes 4 cups, serves 8

15-oz. can low-sodium black beans, drained
    and rinsed
15-oz. can black-eyed peas, drained and rinsed
15¼-oz. can corn, drained
16-oz. jar salsa
Garnish: chopped fresh cilantro

Stir together all ingredients except cilantro; pour into an airtight container. Refrigerate several hours before serving. Garnish, if desired.

Nutrition Per Serving: 234 calories, 1g fat, 0g sat fat, 0mg cholesterol, 575mg sodium, 43g carbohydrate, 10g fiber, 6g sugars, 14g protein.

Texas Caviar

Lisa McGee, *New Brunswick, Canada*

White Bean Hummus

This is a lower-fat hummus that's made with white beans instead of the usual chickpeas. Change up the seasonings as you like...I've sometimes used fresh rosemary instead of cumin and chili powder. Very tasty with pitas and veggies!

Makes 2 cups, serves 8

19-oz. can white kidney beans, drained and rinsed
1 T. fresh parsley, chopped
1 T. lemon juice
1 T. olive oil
¼ t. ground cumin
¼ t. chili powder
1 clove garlic, chopped
salt and pepper to taste

Combine all ingredients in a food processor or blender; process until smooth. Cover and chill for about one hour before serving.

Nutrition Per Serving: 80 calories, 2g fat, 0g sat fat, 0mg cholesterol, 228mg sodium, 11g carbohydrate, 0g fiber, 1g sugars, 4g protein.

Barb Bargdill, *Gooseberry Patch*

Cheesy Tuna Triangles

It's the sweet raisin bread and chopped apple that make these sandwiches stand out from all the rest.

Makes 12 servings

1 T. oil
1 c. apple, cored and chopped
3 T. onion, chopped
7-oz. can albacore tuna, drained
¼ c. chopped walnuts
¼ c. light mayonnaise
2 t. lemon juice
⅛ t. salt
⅛ t. pepper
6 slices raisin bread, toasted and halved diagonally
6 slices reduced-fat sharp Cheddar cheese, halved diagonally

Heat oil in a skillet over medium heat; add apple and onion. Cook, stirring occasionally, about 5 minutes until tender. Remove from heat; transfer to a bowl. Stir in tuna, walnuts, mayonnaise, lemon juice, salt and pepper. Place toast slices on an ungreased baking sheet. Top with tuna mixture and a slice of cheese. Broil 4 to 5 inches from heat for 3 to 4 minutes, or until cheese begins to melt.

Nutrition Per Serving: 121 calories, 7g fat, 2g sat fat, 15mg cholesterol, 217mg sodium, 9g carbohydrate, 1g fiber, 2g sugars, 7g protein.

Cheesy Tuna Triangles

Celeste Pierce, *Overland Park, KS*

Cucumber Tea Sandwiches

I like to think I'm a good cook, but this simple recipe is the one people always request! These dainty sandwiches are one of the few things that my 89-year-old mother still has an appetite for.

Makes 40 servings

2 cucumbers, peeled and thinly sliced
½ c. light sour cream
½ c. light mayonnaise
½ c. non-fat plain yogurt
1 t. dill weed
½ t. onion powder
½ t. seasoned salt
¼ t. garlic powder
⅛ t. kosher salt
20 slices finely-textured whole-grain bread,
    thinly sliced

Place cucumber slices between paper towels; allow to dry for 5 minutes. Mix together remaining ingredients except bread. Spread sour cream mixture over one side of all 20 bread slices. Cover 10 slices with cucumbers; top with remaining bread slices. Quarter each sandwich; arrange on a serving plate. Cover and refrigerate; best served within 6 hours.

Nutrition Per Serving: 50 calories, 2g fat, 0g sat fat, 2mg cholesterol, 121mg sodium, 7g carbohydrate, 1g fiber, 1g sugars, 2g protein.

Celestina Torrez, *Camden, NJ*

Mini Ham & Swiss Frittatas

I first started making these for my toddlers as easy-to-handle mini omelets. My husband thought they would be yummy as appetizers too, so now I serve them when we're watching the big game on TV. They're still a hit with my kids too!

Makes 2 dozen, serves 24

8-oz. pkg. cooked ham, diced
⅔ c. shredded Swiss cheese
¼ c. fresh chives, chopped
pepper to taste
8 eggs, beaten

In a bowl, mix together ham, cheese, chives and pepper; set aside. Spray mini muffin cups with non-stick vegetable oil spray. Fill muffin cups half full with cheese mixture. Spoon in eggs to fill cups. Bake at 375 degrees until golden, about 13 minutes. Serve warm.

Nutrition Per Serving: 49 calories, 3g fat, 1g sat fat, 72mg cholesterol, 176mg sodium, 0g carbohydrate, 0g fiber, 0g sugars, 5g protein.

Kitchen Helper
Prepare the mixture for the frittatas ahead of time and keep refrigerated (up to 24 hours) until ready to pour into the pans.

Mini Ham & Swiss Frittatas

Crispy Zucchini Fritters

Debra Manley, *Bowling Green, OH*

Crispy Zucchini Fritters

These little fritters are so tasty served with ranch dressing for dipping. I even like to warm the dressing just a bit.

Serves 8

4 zucchini, thickly shredded
1 t. salt, divided
2 eggs, beaten
½ t. pepper
½ c. all-purpose flour
3 T. olive oil for frying

Toss zucchini with ½ teaspoon salt. Transfer to a colander and let stand 10 minutes. Drain, pressing out as much liquid as possible. In a large bowl, whisk together eggs, remaining salt and pepper until light and frothy. Whisk in zucchini; stir in flour. Heat oil in a large non-stick skillet over medium-high heat. Drop batter by tablespoonfuls, flattening with the back of spoon. Fry, about 2 minutes on each side, until crisp and golden.

Nutrition Per Serving: 93 calories, 6g fat, 1g sat fat, 47mg cholesterol, 313mg sodium, 6g carbohydrate, 0g fiber, 0g sugars, 3g protein.

Cindy Snyder, *Kittanning, PA*

Cheddar Apple Pie Dip

This is a great appetizer for a fall gathering of friends around a toasty fire. I also like to serve it at family gatherings. I serve it with whole-grain crackers or small pieces of toasted whole-grain bread.

Serves 8

¼ c. brown sugar, packed
¼ t. cinnamon
1 red apple, cored and finely chopped
1 Granny Smith apple, cored and finely chopped
½ c. pecan pieces, coarsely chopped
8-oz. pkg. light cream cheese, softened
1½ c. reduced-fat shredded sharp Cheddar cheese
¼ c. light sour cream

Combine brown sugar and cinnamon in a bowl; stir in apples and pecans. Mix cream cheese and Cheddar cheese; add sour cream, stirring well to blend. Spread mixture in a 9" pie plate; top with apple mixture. Bake, uncovered, at 375 degrees for 20 minutes, or until heated through.

Nutrition Per Serving: 231 calories, 14g fat, 6g sat fat, 30mg cholesterol, 295mg sodium, 18g carbohydrate, 2g fiber, 14g sugars, 9g protein.

Kay Snyder, *Cuba, NY*

Smoky Salmon Spread

My dad would be so proud that I'm sharing this flavorful recipe! You can use it as a dip or spread...either way it is amazing!

Makes about 2 cups, serves 16

16-oz. can salmon, drained
8-oz. pkg. light cream cheese, softened
2 T. lemon juice
2 T. prepared horseradish
1 T. onion, grated
½ t. smoke-flavored cooking sauce
¼ t. salt
¼ c. pistachios, finely chopped

Flake salmon, discarding any skin or bones. Combine all ingredients in a large bowl and mix thoroughly. Refrigerate for several hours before serving. Serve with crackers.

Nutrition Per Serving: 80 calories, 4g fat, 2g sat fat, 31mg cholesterol, 219mg sodium, 2g carbohydrate, 0g fiber, 1g sugars, 8g protein.

Kitchen Helper

Grate onion and keep it in the freezer in small plastic zip-top bags so you have it ready for most any recipe.

Sharon Crider, *Lebanon, MO*

Barbecue Chicken Wings

These wings are really easy to make because you use your slow cooker. Serve on a big serving tray with fresh vegetables cut into bite-size pieces.

Makes 30 servings

3 lbs. trimmed chicken wings
1 c. low-sodium barbecue sauce
½ c. water
2 T. honey
2 t. yellow mustard
1½ t. Worcestershire sauce

Arrange chicken pieces on broiler pan. Broil wings 4 to 5 inches from heat, turning once, about 10 minutes until chicken is golden. Place chicken in a 4-quart slow cooker. Combine barbecue sauce, water, honey, mustard and Worcestershire sauce in a bowl; mix well and pour over chicken. Cover and heat on low setting for 2 to 2 ½ hours.

Nutrition Per Serving: 134 calories, 8g fat, 2g sat fat, 64mg cholesterol, 62mg sodium, 5g carbohydrate, 0g fiber, 4g sugars, 11g protein.

Barbecue Chicken Wings

Mediterranean Sandwiches

Shirl Parsons, *Cape Carteret, NC*

Mediterranean Sandwiches

This is a tasty twist on the "usual" chicken salad sandwich.

Makes 6 servings

4 boneless, skinless chicken breasts
1 t. dried basil
¼ t. salt
¼ t. pepper
1 c. cucumber, chopped
½ c. mayonnaise
¼ c. roasted red pepper, chopped
¼ c. sliced black olives
¼ c. plain yogurt
¼ t. garlic powder
6 kaiser rolls, split
Garnish: mayonnaise, lettuce leaves

Combine chicken, basil, salt and pepper in a stockpot. Cover with water and bring to a boil. Reduce heat and simmer, covered, 10 to 12 minutes until chicken is no longer pink in center. Remove chicken from pan; set aside to cool. Cube chicken and combine with remaining ingredients except rolls and garnish. Toss well to coat. Spread rolls with additional mayonnaise; top with lettuce and chicken salad mixture.

Nutrition Per Serving: 172 calories, 5g fat, 1g sat fat, 34mg cholesterol, 267mg sodium, 17g carbohydrate, 1g fiber, 1g sugars, 15g protein.

Nola Coons, *Gooseberry Patch*

Homebaked Pita Chips

These homemade crispy chips are the best!

Serves 10

6 pita rounds, halved and split
1 T. kosher salt

Cut each pita half into 8 to 12 wedges. Arrange on an aluminum-foil lined baking sheet. Spray chips with non-stick vegetable spray; sprinkle with salt. Broil for 3 to 5 minutes, until golden.

Nutrition Per Serving: 99 calories, 0g fat, 0g sat fat, 0mg cholesterol, 900mg sodium, 20g carbohydrate, 1g fiber, 0g sugars, 3g protein.

Shirl Parsons, *Cape Carteret, NC*

Banana-Mango Soy Smoothies

This smoothie is a favorite of our kids!

Serves 6

2 c. vanilla or plain soy milk
3 bananas, sliced and frozen
6 mangoes, pitted, peeled, cubed and frozen
1 T. honey

Combine all ingredients in a blender. Blend on high setting until smooth and frothy. Pour into tall glasses.

Nutrition Per Serving: 224 calories, 3g fat, 0g sat fat, 0mg cholesterol, 43mg sodium, 50g carbohydrate, 5g fiber, 40g sugars, 5g protein.

Chapter Four

Hearty Soups & Homemade Breads

Cozy up with **Comforting Soups and Breads** that are packed with good-for-you ingredients. Try a bowl of Country Minestrone Soup (only 175 calories per serving!) with a slice of your favorite toasted bread. Grandma's Zucchini Bread is chock-full of nuts and zucchini and is so moist and rich! Curl up with a bowl of Slow-Cooker Chile Verde Soup seasoned with just the right spices. So settle in with some bowls of comfort and slices of homemade goodness that make you feel warm and toasty all day.

Cheryl Donnelly, *Arvada, CO*

Summer Squash Chowder

I love this soup in the late summer and early fall when the gardens are full of produce.

Makes 4 servings

2 slices bacon, chopped
1 onion, finely diced
1 clove garlic, minced
1 yellow or red pepper, finely diced
2 T. all-purpose flour
14¹/₂-oz. can low-sodium vegetable broth, divided
5-oz. can evaporated milk
4 zucchini, diced
2 yellow squash, diced
1 t. white wine Worcestershire sauce
¹/₂ t. hot pepper sauce
³/₄ t. dried thyme
¹/₂ t. salt
1 c. fresh corn kernels
2 T. lemon juice
¹/₂ c. fresh parsley, finely chopped
pepper to taste

In a soup pot over medium heat, cook bacon until crisp. Set aside bacon and drain, reserving drippings in soup pot. Add onion, garlic and yellow or red pepper to soup pot; sauté for 5 minutes. Sprinkle flour evenly over vegetables and cook one minute. Add ¹/₂ cup broth, stirring well to blend. Cook over medium heat until thickened. Pour in remaining broth, milk, zucchini, squash, sauces, thyme and salt. Bring to a boil. Reduce heat and simmer, covered, 15 minutes, stirring occasionally. Add corn to a saucepan; cover with water. Cook over medium heat 5 minutes. Drain and stir into soup mixture. Add reserved bacon, juice and parsley. Heat through and add pepper to taste.

Nutrition Per Serving: 181 calories, 3g fat, 1g sat fat, 6mg cholesterol, 521mg sodium, 32g carbohydrate, 6g fiber, 18g sugars, 10g protein.

Elaine Slabinski, *Monroe Township, NJ*

Creamy Asparagus Soup

This soup is so naturally beautiful and green.

Makes 4 servings

1¹/₂ lbs. asparagus, trimmed and chopped
14¹/₂-oz. can low-sodium chicken broth
1 T. onion, minced
¹/₄ t. salt
¹/₄ t. white pepper
¹/₂ c. 2% milk

Set aside a few asparagus tips for garnish. Combine remaining ingredients except milk in a soup pot over medium heat. Bring to a boil; reduce heat and simmer 5 to 7 minutes, or until asparagus is tender. Working in small batches, ladle asparagus mixture into a blender. Add milk slowly and purée. Return mixture to soup pot and heat through without boiling. Steam or microwave reserved asparagus tips just until tender; use to garnish soup.

Nutrition Per Serving: 60 calories, 1g fat, 1g sat fat, 4mg cholesterol, 213mg sodium, 9g carbohydrate, 4g fiber, 5g sugars, 6g protein.

Creamy Asparagus Soup

Chicken, White Bean & Pasta Soup

Lydia Edgy, *Patterson, MO*

Chicken, White Bean & Pasta Soup

This is such a healthy, satisfying soup. I always feel good when I serve it to my family.

Makes 8 servings

1 onion, chopped
4 carrots, peeled and sliced
4 stalks celery, sliced
2 T. olive oil
4 c. low-sodium chicken broth
3 c. water, divided
2 to 3 boneless, skinless chicken breasts, cooked and diced
2 15½-oz. cans Great Northern beans, drained
6 cherry tomatoes, diced
½ t. dried thyme
½ t. dried rosemary
salt and pepper to taste
1 c. rotini pasta, uncooked
½ lb. baby spinach

In a large saucepan over medium heat, sauté onion, carrots and celery in oil. Add broth and 2 cups water. Bring to a boil; simmer for 10 minutes. Stir in chicken, beans, tomatoes and seasonings. Reduce heat to low; cover and simmer for 25 to 30 minutes. Return to a boil; stir in pasta. Cook until pasta is tender, about 10 minutes. Add remaining water if soup is too thick. Stir in spinach and cook for 2 minutes, or until wilted.

Nutrition Per Serving: 319 calories, 6g fat, 1g sat fat, 43 mg cholesterol, 297mg sodium, 40g carbohydrate, 8g fiber, 5g sugars, 26g protein.

Kristin Turman, *Jackson, TN*

Yummy Banana-Nut Bread

I love to make this for breakfast on a cool morning, or sometimes for an evening snack. Whenever I serve it, the family loves it and asks for more!

Makes one loaf, serves 8

¼ c. butter
½ c. sugar
1 egg, beaten
1 t. vanilla extract
2 to 3 bananas, mashed
1 c. all-purpose flour
1 t. baking soda
½ c. chopped pecans or walnuts
Optional: ½ c. blueberries

Blend butter and sugar together until creamy; stir in egg and vanilla. Add mashed bananas and stir well; fold in remaining ingredients. Pour into a greased 9"x5" loaf pan. Bake at 350 degrees for 30 to 35 minutes, until golden.

Nutrition Per Serving: 238 calories, 12g fat, 4g sat fat, 39mg cholesterol, 168mg sodium, 32g carbohydrate, 2g fiber, 16g sugars, 3g protein.

Colleen Pancari, *Vineland, NJ*

Vegetable Beef Soup

Every country kitchen should have an easy, delicious recipe for vegetable beef soup...this is mine!

Serves 6

1 lb. stew beef cubes
3 14¹/₂-oz. cans low-sodium beef broth
2 16-oz. pkgs. frozen mixed vegetables
14¹/₂-oz. can whole tomatoes
16-oz. pkg. wide egg noodles, uncooked and
    divided

Combine all ingredients except noodles in a slow cooker. Cover and cook on low setting for 4 hours. Increase to high setting; cover and cook for 5 additional hours. About 20 minutes before serving, stir in half the noodles, or desired amount, reserving the rest for another recipe. Cover and cook an additional 15 to 20 minutes, until noodles are tender.

Nutrition Per Serving: 527 calories, 8g fat, 3g sat fat, 112mg cholesterol, 312mg sodium, 79g carbohydrate, 10g fiber, 3g sugars, 35g protein.

Kitchen Helper

Convert your favorite stovetop soup recipe to fix & forget in a slow cooker. Most soups that simmer for one to 2 hours will be done in 4 to 5 hours on high in a slow cooker.

Vickie, *Gooseberry Patch*

Cheddar-Dill Corn Muffins

These dressed-up corn muffins are scrumptious and simple to make.

Makes one dozen, serves 12

1 c. cornmeal
1 c. all-purpose flour
¹/₃ c. sugar
2¹/₂ t. baking powder
¹/₂ t. baking soda
¹/₄ t. salt
1 egg
³/₄ c. skim milk
1 c. shredded low-fat sharp Cheddar cheese
1 c. corn, thawed if frozen
¹/₄ c. butter, melted
3 T. fresh dill, minced, or 1 T. dill weed

In a large bowl, mix cornmeal, flour, sugar, baking powder, baking soda and salt; set aside. In a separate bowl, whisk together egg and milk; stir in remaining ingredients. Add egg mixture to cornmeal mixture; stir just until moistened. Spoon batter into 12 greased or paper-lined muffin cups, filling cups ²/₃ full. Bake at 400 degrees for about 20 minutes, until golden and a toothpick inserted in the center tests clean. Cool muffins in tin on a wire rack for 10 minutes before turning out of tin. Serve warm or at room temperature.

Nutrition Per Serving: 187 calories, 6g fat, 4g sat fat, 31mg cholesterol, 260mg sodium, 27g carbohydrate, 1g fiber, 7g sugars, 6g protein.

Cheddar-Dill Corn Muffins

Cranberry-Carrot Loaf

Diane Widmer, *Blue Island, IL*

Cranberry-Carrot Loaf

My grandmother gave me this recipe. I've updated it by reducing the sugar, replacing the oil with applesauce and adding cranberries. I think you'll agree it's still packed with old-fashioned goodness!

Makes one loaf, serves 8

2 c. all-purpose flour
³/₄ c. sugar
1¹/₂ t. baking powder
1¹/₂ t. baking soda
¹/₄ t. salt
¹/₂ t. cinnamon
¹/₂ c. carrot, peeled and shredded
¹/₃ c. light sour cream
¹/₄ c. unsweetened applesauce
¹/₄ c. water
2 eggs, lightly beaten
1 c. frozen cranberries

Grease the bottom of a 9"x5" loaf pan; set aside. In a large bowl, mix together flour, sugar, baking powder, baking soda, salt and cinnamon. Stir in carrot to coat. Make a well in center of flour mixture; add sour cream, applesauce, water and eggs. Stir until combined. Slowly stir in cranberries. Spoon batter into pan. Bake on center oven rack at 350 degrees for 60 minutes, or until a toothpick inserted in the center comes out clean. Cool loaf in pan for 15 minutes. Remove to a rack and cool completely.

Nutrition Per Serving: 233 calories, 3g fat, 1g sat fat, 52mg cholesterol, 340mg sodium, 47g carbohydrate, 2g fiber, 21g sugars, 5g protein.

Lorrie Haskell, *Lyndeborough, NH*

Lorrie's 2-Bean Chili

You'll love this meatless chili!

Makes 6 servings

¹/₂ lb. mushrooms, chopped
1 onion, chopped
3 stalks celery, chopped
1 green pepper, chopped
1 red pepper, chopped
Optional: 1 jalapeño pepper, seeded and chopped
1 T. olive oil
4 cloves garlic, minced
2 t. ground cumin
1¹/₂ t. dried oregano
28-oz. can diced tomatoes
16-oz. can low-sodium red beans, drained and rinsed
16-oz. can low-sodium black beans, drained and rinsed
1 carrot, peeled and chopped
¹/₂ c. low-sodium barbecue sauce
¹/₂ c. water
¹/₄ t. chili powder

In a large skillet over medium heat, cook mushrooms, onion, celery and peppers in olive oil until tender. Add garlic, cumin and oregano; cook and stir for 2 to 3 minutes longer. Drain; transfer to a slow cooker. Stir in tomatoes with juice and remaining ingredients. Cover and cook on low setting for 8 hours.

Nutrition Per Serving: 268 calories, 3g fat, 1g sat fat, 0mg cholesterol, 469mg sodium, 48g carbohydrate, 14g fiber, 17g sugars, 13g protein.

Hobo Stew

Char Pletcher, *Lone Grove, OK*

Hobo Stew

This recipe has been a family favorite for years! I love that there are so many veggies in it.

Serves 10

1 lb. ground beef
1 onion, diced
1/4 t. seasoned salt with onion & garlic
4 potatoes, peeled and cubed
3 carrots, peeled and sliced
28-oz. can whole tomatoes, broken up
15 1/4-oz. can no-salt-added corn
15-oz. can no-sodium black beans
14 1/2-oz. can green beans
1 T. onion soup mix
0.87-oz. pkg. brown gravy mix

Brown beef with onion and seasoning in a stockpot over medium heat. Drain; add remaining ingredients and enough water to cover. Bring to a boil; reduce heat. Simmer until vegetables are tender, about 30 to 40 minutes, adding a little more water if needed.

Nutrition Per Serving: 260 calories, 5g fat, 2g sat fat, 30mg cholesterol, 594mg sodium, 40g carbohydrate, 8g fiber, 5g sugars, 16g protein.

Suzanne Williams, *Azusa, CA*

Sheila's Corn Soup

When my daughter became a vegetarian, this was one of the first recipes she shared with me. If you prefer, use evaporated milk or regular milk instead of the coconut milk. This soup freezes well...very handy when sweet corn is fresh!

Makes 6 servings

1/2 c. yellow onion, diced
1 T. olive oil
5 cloves garlic, minced
1 T. curry powder
sea salt and pepper to taste
2 to 3 c. corn
14-oz. can vegetable broth
14-oz. can coconut milk

In a large saucepan over medium-low heat, sauté onion in olive oil until tender, about 5 minutes. Add garlic and sauté until fragrant, 2 to 3 minutes. Stir in curry powder and season well with salt and pepper; cook another 2 to 3 minutes. Stir in corn, broth and milk. Cover and simmer over low heat for 25 minutes. With an immersion blender, purée soup to desired consistency.

Nutrition Per Serving: 205 calories, 17g fat, 13g sat fat, 0mg cholesterol, 167mg sodium, 15g carbohydrate, 2g fiber, 3g sugars, 3g protein.

Madge Shepard, *Franklin, NC*

Madge's Beefy Chili

A good bowl of chili is appreciated year 'round, but especially in chilly weather. Serve with a cast-iron skillet of cornbread or crisp corn chips...yum!

Makes 8 servings

2 lbs. ground beef
1 green pepper, chopped
1 onion, chopped
16-oz. can kidney beans
15¹/₂-oz. can diced tomatoes
10-oz. can chili-style diced tomatoes with green chiles
8-oz. can low-sodium tomato sauce
1-oz. pkg. chili seasoning

In a large skillet, brown beef, pepper and onion together; drain. Mix beef mixture with remaining ingredients in a slow cooker. Cover and cook on low setting for 2 to 4 hours, until hot and well blended.

Nutrition Per Serving: 299 calories, 12g fat, 5g sat fat, 74mg cholesterol, 560mg sodium, 19g carbohydrate, 6g fiber, 6g sugars, 27g protein.

Susan Rodgers, *Mohnton, PA*

Gran-Gran's Sweet Bread

This recipe makes plenty of loaves to freeze. I cut the loaves into 10 slices each.

Makes 6 loaves, serves 60

¹/₂ c. butter, softened
¹/₂ c. shortening
1¹/₂ c. sugar
3 eggs, beaten
2 t. vanilla extract
2 env. active dry yeast
1 c. warm water
8 c. all-purpose flour
¹/₂ t. salt
2 c. warm skim milk
16-oz. pkg. raisins
3 T. butter, melted
2 T. sugar

Blend together butter and shortening in a large bowl. Gradually add sugar, eggs and vanilla, beating well after each addition. Dissolve yeast in warm water (110 to 115 degrees) in a cup; let stand 5 minutes. Whisk together flour and salt. Gradually stir flour and salt with a large wooden spoon into butter mixture alternately with yeast mixture and warm milk. Mix well; stir in raisins. Turn dough out onto a floured surface. Knead, adding additional flour until dough is smooth and elastic. Return dough to bowl. Lightly spray dough with non-stick vegetable spray; cover with wax paper and a tea towel. Let rise 6 to 8 hours or overnight, until double in bulk. Punch down; divide into 6 equal portions and place in 6 greased 9"x5" loaf pans. Cover and let rise again 4 to 6 hours, until double in bulk. Drizzle melted butter over loaves; sprinkle each loaf with 2 teaspoons sugar. Bake at 350 degrees for 30 minutes, or until a toothpick inserted in center comes out clean. Cool on wire racks.

Nutrition Per Serving: 145 calories, 4g fat, 2g sat fat, 15mg cholesterol, 28mg sodium, 25g carbohydrate, 1g fiber, 10g sugars, 3g protein.

Gran-Gran's Sweet Bread

Mary Muchowicz, *Elk Grove Village, IL*

White Chicken Chili

I love to make this soup to serve on a cold winter night.

Makes 10 servings

2 16-oz. cans navy beans, drained and rinsed
4 14½-oz. cans low-sodium chicken broth
1 onion, chopped
2 cloves garlic, minced
1 T. ground cumin
1 T. dried oregano
1 t. salt
1 T. white pepper
¼ t. ground cloves
1 c. water
5 c. cooked chicken, chopped
2 4-oz. cans chopped green chiles
Garnish: shredded Monterey Jack cheese,
    plain Greek yogurt

Combine all ingredients except garnish in a large slow cooker. Cover and cook on low setting for 8 to 10 hours, or on high setting for 4 to 5 hours. Garnish as desired.

Nutrition Per Serving: 273 calories, 4g fat, 1g sat fat, 53mg cholesterol, 412mg sodium, 28g carbohydrate, 10g fiber, 1g sugars, 30g protein.

Happy Presentation

Serve this rich soup in deep mugs
with a sprinkling of your favorite
cheese on top and a slice of
homemade cornbread.

Eleanor Dionne, *Beverly, MA*

Italian Lentil & Vegetable Stew

Growing up in an Italian family, we ate a lot of vegetable dishes. We called it "peasant food" and boy, was it yummy. My mom always made some kind of homemade stew or soup every Monday in the winter. This slow-cooker recipe is still a favorite of mine.

Makes 8 servings

1 c. dried lentils, uncooked
3 c. water
2 c. marinara sauce
1¼ lbs. butternut squash, peeled and cut
    into 1-inch cubes
½ lb. green beans, trimmed and cut into 1-inch
    lengths
1 green pepper, cut into 1-inch squares
1 small potato, peeled and cut into 1-inch cubes
¾ c. onion, chopped
1 t. garlic, minced
1 T. olive oil

Combine lentils and water in a large slow cooker. Add remaining ingredients except olive oil; stir. Cover and cook on low setting for 8 hours, or until lentils and vegetables are tender. At serving time, stir in olive oil; ladle into bowls.

Nutrition Per Serving: 192 calories, 3g fat, 0g sat fat, 0mg cholesterol, 269mg sodium, 34g carbohydrate, 11g fiber, 7g sugars, 9g protein.

Italian Lentil & Vegetable Stew

Miss Sallie's Light Cornbread

Mary Little, *Franklin, TN*

Miss Sallie's Light Cornbread

We have enjoyed this yummy bread for many years at family gatherings.

Makes 2 loaves, serves 16

¼ c. oil, divided
3 c. self-rising cornmeal
1 c. self-rising flour
1¼ c. sugar
2 c. buttermilk
1 c. 2 % milk

Divide oil between two 9"x5" loaf pans. Heat pans in a 375-degree oven for about 5 minutes; remove from oven. In a large bowl, mix together cornmeal, flour and sugar; set aside. Combine milks in a small bowl. Tilt pans to coat with oil; pour remaining oil from both pans into milk mixture. Add milk mixture to cornmeal mixture; stir well. Divide batter evenly between pans. Bake at 375 degrees for 55 minutes. Cool bread before slicing.

Nutrition Per Serving: 230 calories, 4g fat, 1g sat fat, 2mg cholesterol, 508mg sodium, 43g carbohydrate, 2g fiber, 18g sugars, 4g protein.

Amy Thomason Hunt, *Traphill, NC*

Scrumptious Pumpkin Bread

My husband and nephews love pumpkin rolls and this is an easy version that I love to make.

Makes one loaf, serves 8

1 c. canned pumpkin
1 c. plus 2 T. sugar, divided
½ c. brown sugar, packed
4 egg whites, divided
½ c. skim milk
¼ c. canola oil
2 c. all-purpose flour
2½ t. baking powder
2 t. pumpkin pie spice
¼ t. salt
1 c. walnut pieces
8-oz. pkg. Neufchâtel cheese, softened

Combine pumpkin, one cup sugar, brown sugar, 3 egg whites, milk and oil in a large bowl. In a separate bowl, sift together flour, baking powder, pumpkin pie spice and salt; stir into pumpkin mixture just until moistened. Stir in walnut pieces. Blend together Neufchâtel cheese, remaining sugar and egg white until smooth. Spoon half the pumpkin mixture into a greased 9"x5" loaf pan. Spoon Neufchâtel cheese mixture over pumpkin layer; cover with remaining pumpkin mixture. Bake at 350 degrees for one hour, or until a wooden toothpick inserted near the center comes out clean. Cool in pan for 10 minutes, then remove bread from pan to a wire rack to finish cooling.

Nutrition Per Serving: 531 calories, 23g fat, 5g sat fat, 21mg cholesterol, 210mg sodium, 73g carbohydrate, 3g fiber, 45g sugars, 11g protein.

Patti Bogetti, *Magnolia, DE*

Blue-Ribbon Crab & Asparagus Chowder

If you like asparagus, you will love this amazing chowder! The recipe has become a tradition at my friend's Barn Bash every fall. Everyone always asks that I bring it every year. Recently, I won the blue ribbon at the state fair in the Chili vs. Chowder Cook-off, yee-haw!

Serves 10

1/2 c. butter
1 sweet onion, chopped
2 carrots, peeled and chopped
3 stalks celery, chopped
1 t. salt
1/2 t. pepper
1/4 c. all-purpose flour
4 c. water
1/2 t. nutmeg
1 t. seafood seasoning
1 T. chicken bouillon granules
3 redskin potatoes, peeled and cubed
4 c. whole milk
2 t. fresh parsley, chopped
3 c. asparagus, trimmed and chopped
1 lb. crabmeat
Optional: additional milk

Melt butter in a large stockpot over medium heat; add onion, carrots, celery, salt and pepper. Continue to cook until vegetables are softened, about 10 minutes. Stir in flour to coat vegetables. Slowly whisk in water; stir in nutmeg, seasoning, bouillon and potatoes. Bring to a boil; reduce heat and simmer, covered, 10 minutes or until potatoes are tender. Add milk, parsley and asparagus. Simmer 10 minutes longer. Gently fold in crabmeat. Heat through. If chowder is too thick, thin with more milk, if desired.

Nutrition Per Serving: 215 calories, 8g fat, 5g sat fat, 66mg cholesterol, 696mg sodium, 21g carbohydrate, 3g fiber, 8g sugars, 14g protein.

Robyn Stroh, *Calera, AL*

Daddy's Veggie Soup

One week my husband requested vegetable or cabbage soup. So I came up with this delicious soup that had all kinds of veggies and some protein too. He loved it and now I make it all the time!

Makes 15 servings

1 lb. extra-lean ground beef
2 onions, chopped
16-oz. pkg. baby carrots, cut into thirds
2 14 1/2-oz. cans green beans, drained
1 head cabbage, chopped
10-oz. pkg. frozen corn
2 46-oz. cans cocktail vegetable juice, divided
salt and pepper to taste

In a large Dutch oven over medium heat, brown beef with onions; drain. Add carrots. Reduce heat to medium-low; cover and cook for 10 to 15 minutes, until carrots are crisp-tender. Add beans, cabbage and corn; pour in one can vegetable juice. Increase heat slightly. Cover and simmer, stirring occasionally, for 30 minutes, or until cabbage has cooked down. Add remaining can of juice; continue to cook for 30 more minutes. Season to taste with salt and pepper.

Nutrition Per Serving: 126 calories, 3g fat, 1g sat fat, 17mg cholesterol, 337mg sodium, 17g carbohydrate, 5g fiber, 8g sugars, 10g protein.

Lynn Williams, *Muncie, IN*

Soft Sesame Bread Sticks

Delicious with just about any soup or salad!

Makes one dozen, serves 12

1¼ c. all-purpose flour
2 t. sugar
1½ t. baking powder
½ t. salt
⅔ c. 2% milk
2 T. butter, melted
2 t. sesame seed

In a small bowl, combine flour, sugar, baking powder and salt. Gradually add milk; stir to form a soft dough. Turn dough onto a floured surface; knead gently 3 to 4 times. Roll into a 10-inch by 5½ inch rectangle; cut into 12 bread sticks. Place butter in a 13"x9" baking pan; coat bread sticks in butter and sprinkle with sesame seed. Bake at 450 degrees for 14 to 18 minutes, until golden.

Nutrition Per Serving: 70 calories, 2g fat, 1g sat fat, 5mg cholesterol, 166mg sodium, 11g carbohydrates, 1g fiber, 1g sugars, 2g protein.

Soft Sesame Bread Sticks

Country Minestrone Soup

Erica Clopton, *Fort Worth, TX*

Country Minestrone Soup

This tasty recipe was given to me by my mother-in-law. She is a great cook!

Serves 8

2 T. canola oil
1 c. onion, chopped
1/2 c. celery, sliced
14 1/2-oz. can beef broth
10-oz. can low-sodium bean with bacon soup
2 3/4 c. water
1 t. dried basil
1/2 t. salt
1/2 t. pepper
14 1/2-oz. can diced tomatoes
8-oz. pkg. elbow macaroni, uncooked
1 c. cabbage, chopped
1 c. zucchini, cubed
1 c. yellow squash, cubed
1/2 t. beef bouillon granules
2 slices bacon, crisply cooked and diced

In a heavy skillet, add canola oil and sauté onion and celery until tender. Stir in broth, soup, water, basil, salt, pepper and tomatoes. Bring to a boil; reduce heat and simmer 10 minutes. Add remaining ingredients except reserved bacon. Simmer for 10 minutes, or until macaroni and vegetables are tender. Add bacon on top.

Nutrition Per Serving: 175 calories, 5g fat, 1g sat fat, 3mg cholesterol, 591mg sodium, 27g carbohydrate, 3g fiber, 4g sugars, 6g protein.

Nancy Campbell, *Bellingham, WA*

Veggie Patch Stew

This yummy stew uses just about every vegetable from our garden. That is how it got its name!

Makes 6 servings

3 zucchini, sliced
3 yellow squash, sliced
2 onions, chopped
2 tomatoes, chopped
1 eggplant, peeled and cubed
1 green pepper, chopped
1 clove garlic, minced
1 T. butter, softened
1 t. hot pepper sauce
1/2 t. curry powder
1 t. chili powder
salt and pepper to taste
Garnish: shredded mozzarella cheese

Place all vegetables in a large Dutch oven over low heat. Stir in remaining ingredients except cheese. Cover and simmer for one hour, stirring frequently. Do not add any liquid, as vegetables make their own juices. Top portions with cheese before serving if desired.

Nutrition Per Serving: 94 calories, 3g total fat, 1g sat fat, 5mg cholesterol, 45mg sodium, 17g carbohydrate, 6g fiber, 11g sugars, 4g protein.

Kathie Poritz, *Burlington, WI*

Generations Rhubarb Bread

I've had this recipe for years. Now, I have my grandchildren helping me harvest rhubarb!

Makes 2 small loaves, serves 16

1¹/₂ c. rhubarb, finely diced
³/₄ c. brown sugar, packed
³/₄ c. sugar
1 c. skim milk
1 t. vinegar
2¹/₂ c. all-purpose flour
¹/₂ c. oil
1 egg, beaten
1 t. baking soda
1 t. salt
1 t. vanilla extract
Optional: ¹/₂ c. chopped nuts
Topping

Sprinkle rhubarb with sugars; set aside. Stir together milk and vinegar. Add remaining ingredients except nuts; stir until thoroughly blended. Stir in rhubarb mixture and nuts, if using. Mix well and pour into 2 greased and floured 9"x5" loaf pans. Sprinkle with Topping. Bake at 350 degrees for 50 to 60 minutes, until toothpick tests clean.

TOPPING:

¹/₄ c. sugar
1 t. cinnamon
1 T. butter

Mix ingredients with a fork until crumbly.

Nutrition Per Serving: 237 calories, 8g fat, 1g sat fat, 14mg cholesterol, 241mg sodium, 39g carbohydrate, 1g fiber, 23g sugars, 3g protein.

Matt McCurdy, *Saint Petersburg, FL*

Rosemary-Sea Salt Bread

After my girlfriend moved out of state, I needed to learn how to cook and bake! This is a recipe I make often now.

Makes one loaf, serves 12

4 c. bread flour
2 t. active dry yeast
2 T. fresh rosemary, chopped and divided
2 t. sea salt, divided
2 t. extra-virgin olive oil, divided
2 c. warm water
2 t. cornmeal

In a large bowl, combine flours, yeast, one tablespoon rosemary, one teaspoon salt and one teaspoon olive oil. Heat water until very warm, about 110 to 115 degrees; add to flour mixture. Stir together until well blended; cover with plastic wrap. To allow flavor to develop, let stand at room temperature for about one hour, then refrigerate overnight up to 4 days. Before baking, let bowl stand at room temperature for one hour. Turn out dough onto a lightly floured surface; give dough a stretch or two. Line a baking sheet with parchment paper; sprinkle with cornmeal. Shape dough into a round loaf and place on baking sheet. Combine remaining salt, olive oil and rosemary in a small bowl; brush over dough. Spritz a little water into preheated oven. Bake at 475 degrees for 30 minutes; reduce to 400 degrees and bake for 10 additional minutes. Remove loaf to a wire rack. Cool completely before slicing.

Nutrition Per Serving: 175 calories, 2g fat, 0g sat fat, 0mg cholesterol, 394mg sodium, 34g carbohydrate, 1g fiber, 0g sugars, 6g protein.

Mary Lou Thomas, Portland, ME

Lenten Mushroom-Barley Soup

A warm and comforting soup for a chilly evening. Garnish with some plain yogurt.

Makes 6 servings

2 14-oz. cans low-sodium vegetable broth
2$^1/_2$ c. plus 2 T. water, divided
$^3/_4$ c. quick-cooking barley, uncooked
$^1/_2$ c. onion, chopped
2 cloves garlic, minced

1 T. fresh basil, chopped
$^1/_8$ t. pepper
$^1/_2$ t. Worcestershire sauce
3 c. sliced mushrooms
$^1/_2$ c. carrot, peeled and shredded
2 T. cornstarch
Garnish: chopped fresh parsley

In a large saucepan over high heat, bring vegetable broth and 2$^1/_2$ cups water to a boil. Stir in uncooked barley, onion, garlic, basil, pepper and Worcestershire sauce. Simmer for 5 minutes. Stir in mushrooms and carrot. Cover and simmer for about 5 minutes more, until barley is tender. In a small bowl, combine cornstarch and remaining water; stir into soup. Cook and stir until bubbly and slightly thickened. Cook and stir 2 minutes more. Serve individual bowls sprinkled with parsley.

Nutrition Per Serving: 124 calories, 0g fat, 0g sat fat, 0mg cholesterol, 92mg sodium, 27g carbohydrate, 5g fiber, 3g sugars, 4g protein.

Brandi Howell, *Owego, NY*

Brandi's Ultimate Tex-Mex Soup

During the winter months, my husband and I like to retreat to the couch, enjoy a bowl of this comforting soup and watch a movie.

Serves 8

1 T. olive oil
1 c. onion, diced
1 carrot, peeled and finely grated
1 T. ancho chili powder
1 T. garlic, minced
1½ t. ground cumin
1 t. dried oregano
salt and pepper to taste

4 c. low-sodium vegetable broth
13-oz. can chicken, drained
1 c. frozen corn, thawed
15-oz. can fire-roasted diced tomatoes
28-oz. can black beans, drained and rinsed
15-oz. can garbanzo beans, drained and rinsed
Garnish: plain Greek yogurt, chopped fresh cilantro, lime wedges

Heat oil in a large stockpot over medium-high heat. Sauté onion in oil until golden and tender, 5 to 8 minutes. Add carrot and seasonings; cook one to 2 minutes. Add broth, chicken, corn, tomatoes with juice and beans. Cook over low heat for 25 to 30 minutes. Garnish as desired.

Nutrition Per Serving: 282 calories, 7g fat, 1g sat fat, 29mg cholesterol, 599mg sodium, 35g carbohydrate, 12g fiber, 5g sugars, 20g protein.

Brandi's Ultimate Tex-Mex Soup

Becky Holsinger, *Belpre, OH*

Sheila's Awesome Chicken Noodle Soup

I got this recipe from a co-worker after she had brought this in for a luncheon. I loved it! I took it to a church dinner, there weren't any leftovers to bring home. It really is the best chicken noodle soup I've ever had...and everyone always asks for the recipe!

Makes 10 servings

1½ t. Italian seasoning
1½ t. dried basil
1 t. garlic salt
1 t. salt
1 t. pepper
4 boneless, skinless chicken breasts, cubed
³/₄ c. butter, divided
4 stalks celery, finely chopped
½ onion, finely chopped
1 c. baby carrots, finely chopped
48-oz. low-sodium chicken broth
12-oz. pkg. frozen egg needles, uncooked
32-oz. low-sodium chicken broth, divided

Combine seasonings in a shallow bowl. Coat chicken cubes with seasonings; set aside. Melt ¼ cup butter in a skillet over medium heat. Add chicken and cook until golden, stirring often. Transfer cooked chicken with pan drippings to a stockpot; add vegetables and larger container of broth. Simmer over medium heat until vegetables are tender, about 15 minutes. Stir in frozen noodles and remaining butter. Simmer for 30 to 40 minutes, until noodles are cooked. As broth is absorbed by noodles, add remaining broth from small container as needed.

Nutrition Per Serving: 326 calories, 18g fat, 10g sat fat, 115mg cholesterol, 605mg sodium, 13g carbohydrate, 1g fiber, 1g sugars, 28g protein.

Kitchen Helper

If you make your own chicken broth, freeze it in small containers to use in soups and other recipes. You can also do this with purchased broth.

That Yummy Bread

Francie Stutzman, *Dayton, OH*

That Yummy Bread

*Homemade bread with a savory herb filling...
really unforgettable!*

Makes 2 loaves, serves 20

1 c. skim milk
2 T. sugar
¼ c. butter
2½ t. salt
1 c. water
2 envs. active dry yeast
7 c. all-purpose flour, divided
2 eggs, beaten and divided
Herb Filling
1 T. butter, melted

In a medium saucepan, heat milk just to boiling; stir in sugar, shortening and salt. Cool to lukewarm and set aside. Heat water until warm (110 to 115 degrees); add yeast, stir to dissolve and add to milk mixture. Pour into a large bowl and add 4 cups flour; stir and beat. Gradually add remaining flour; stir. Let dough rest 10 minutes; turn dough out onto a floured surface and knead until smooth. Place dough in a greased bowl, turning to coat. Cover and let rise in a warm place (85 degrees), away from drafts, until doubled in bulk. Punch down dough; shape into 2 balls. Roll out each ball into a ¼-inch-thick 15"x9" rectangle. Brush with 2 tablespoons egg, reserving remainder for filling. Spread Herb Filling to one inch from edges of dough; roll up jelly-roll style, starting at short edge. Pinch edges to seal; place in 2 greased 9"x5" loaf pans, seam-side down. Brush with butter; cover and let rise in a warm place 55 minutes. Slash tops of loaves with a knife; bake at 375 degrees for one hour. Let cool before slicing.

HERB FILLING:

2 c. fresh parsley, chopped
2 c. green onions, chopped
1 clove garlic, minced
2 T. butter
¾ t. salt
**pepper and hot pepper
sauce to taste**

Sauté parsley, onions and garlic in butter; cool slightly and add reserved egg from main recipe. Add salt, pepper and hot pepper sauce.

Nutrition Per Serving: 217 calories, 5g fat, 3g sat fat, 30mg cholesterol, 399mg sodium, 36g carbohydrate, 2g fiber, 2g sugars, 6g protein.

> ～ **Healthy Fact** ～
>
> Parsley is an herb that can be used in so many ways. Used fresh, it makes a lovely garnish. In breads, soups and other recipes it adds flavor, color, and Vitamins K, C and A.

Amanda Fox, *South Weber, UT*

Tex-Mex Quinoa Stew

My entire family loves this hearty soup!

Makes 8 servings

1 lb. boneless, skinless chicken breasts
14¹/₂-oz. can diced tomatoes, drained
11-oz. can corn
2 cloves garlic, minced
1 c. quinoa, uncooked
1 t. chili powder
1 t. ground cumin
¹/₄ t. paprika
¹/₄ t. dried minced onion
¹/₂ c. non-fat plain Greek yogurt
1 c. reduced-fat shredded Cheddar cheese

Place chicken in a slow cooker. Top with tomatoes, undrained corn, garlic, quinoa and seasonings. Cover and cook on low setting for about 7 hours, until chicken is very tender. Remove chicken to a plate. Using 2 forks, shred chicken and stir back into stew. Serve stew in bowls, topped with a dollop of yogurt and a sprinkle of cheese.

Nutrition Per Serving: 224 calories, 3g fat, 1g sat fat, 35mg cholesterol, 352mg sodium, 25g carbohydrate, 3g fiber, 3g sugars, 24g protein.

Lawrie Currin, *Dillon, NC*

Sassy Squash Blossoms

These squash patties are golden and crispy. Serve them with a dollop of plain yogurt.

Makes one dozen, serves 12

3 c. yellow squash, shredded
²/₃ c. biscuit baking mix
¹/₄ c. butter, melted
¹/₄ t. salt
¹/₈ t. pepper
2 eggs, beaten
¹/₄ c. sweet onion, chopped
oil for frying

Place squash in a colander; press out any liquid. Combine baking mix, butter, salt, pepper and eggs. Stir in squash and onion. Heat about ¹/₂ inch of oil in a skillet over medium-high heat. Form squash mixture into patties or drop by tablespoonfuls into hot oil. Cook, turning once, until golden on both sides. Remove from skillet and place on paper towels to drain.

Nutrition Per Serving: 111 calories, 9g fat, 3g sat fat, 41mg cholesterol, 181mg sodium, 6g carbohydrate, 0g fiber, 1g sugars, 2g protein.

Beth Kramer, *Port Saint Lucie, FL*

Crockery Black Bean Soup

This rich soup is filled with all kinds of healthy goodness! You can use canned beans instead of dried if you like, but be sure they are drained before you add them to the mixture. Then you can decrease the cooking time in the slow cooker by 2 hours.

Serves 6

1 T. olive oil
2 red onions, chopped
1 red pepper, chopped
1 green pepper, chopped
4 cloves garlic, minced

4 t. ground cumin
16-oz. pkg. dried black beans
1 T. canned chopped chipotle chiles
7 c. hot water
2 T. lime juice
1 t. kosher salt
1/4 t. pepper
1 c. plain low-fat yogurt
1/2 c. plum tomatoes, chopped and seeded
Garnish: lime wedges, chopped cilantro, sliced
    cherry tomatoes

Heat oil in a skillet over medium-high heat. Add onions and peppers; sauté until tender. Stir in garlic and cumin; cook one minute. Use a slotted spoon to transfer mixture to a slow cooker. Add beans, chiles and hot water. Cover and cook on high setting for 6 hours. Transfer 2 cups bean mixture to a blender; purée until smooth. Return mixture to slow cooker; stir in remaining ingredients. Garnish as desired.

Nutrition Per Serving: 224 calories, 3g fat, 1g sat fat, 35mg cholesterol, 352mg sodium, 25g carbohydrate, 3g fiber, 3g sugars, 24g protein.

Happy Presentation
·················· ✳ ··················

Serve this dark, rich black bean soup in small white bowls. Place the bowls on a red plate or tray and tuck a brown-and-white striped napkin under each bowl.

Mary Patenaude, *Griswold, CT*

Fresh Strawberry Bread

Serve this delicious bread with a dab of homemade strawberry jam or cream cheese.

Makes 2 loaves, serves 16

3 c. all-purpose flour
2 c. sugar
1½ t. cinnamon
1 t. baking soda
4 eggs, beaten
1 c. oil
2 c. strawberries, hulled and diced
Optional: 1¼ c. chopped nuts

In a bowl, combine flour, sugar, cinnamon baking soda and salt. In a separate bowl, whisk together eggs and oil; fold in strawberries. Gradually add egg mixture to flour mixture; stir until just moistened. Add nuts, if using. Pour batter into 2 greased and floured 9"x5" loaf pans. Bake at 350 degrees for one hour.

Nutrition Per Serving: 327 calories, 15g fat, 1g sat fat, 47mg cholesterol, 97mg sodium, 44g carbohydrate, 1g fiber, 25g sugars, 4g protein.

Wendy Reaume, *Ontario, Canada*

West African Chicken Soup

I had a friend long ago who used to make this delicious soup with flavors of tomato, chicken and curry. It's always been well-loved by all.

Makes 6 servings

2 boneless, skinless chicken breasts, cubed
1 c. onion, chopped
1 T. garlic, minced
1 T. olive oil
1½ t. curry powder
½ t. pepper
28-oz. can stewed tomatoes
3 c. low-sodium chicken broth
3 T. creamy peanut butter
3 T. no-salt tomato paste
Garnish: chopped peanuts

In a large saucepan over medium heat, combine chicken, onion, garlic and olive oil. Sauté until chicken is golden and juices run clear when pierced. Stir in seasonings; cook for another minute. Stir in tomatoes with juice and remaining ingredients. Reduce heat to low; cover and simmer for 10 to 15 minutes. Garnish as desired.

Nutrition Per Serving: 229 calories, 9g fat, 2g sat fat, 57mg cholesterol, 408mg sodium, 15g carbohydrate, 2g fiber, 7g sugars, 24g protein.

West African Chicken Soup

Claire Bertram, *Lexington, KY*

Down-Home Soup Beans

There is nothing better than bean soup!

Serves 8

1 lb. dried Great Northern or pinto beans
12 c. water
1 to 1½ c. cooked ham, diced
1 onion, diced
1 c. baby carrots, sliced
1 clove garlic, minced
¼ t. red pepper flakes
½ t. salt
1 t. pepper

Combine all ingredients in a large Dutch oven; bring to a boil. Reduce heat and simmer, stirring occasionally, until beans are very tender and beginning to pop, 1½ to 2 hours. Add a little more water while simmering, if needed to make sure beans are just covered. Remove from heat. Transfer 2 cups of beans to a bowl and coarsely mash with a fork. Return mashed beans to pot; stir to combine and heat through.

Nutrition Per Serving: 235 calories, 1g fat, 0g sat fat, 5mg cholesterol, 374mg sodium, 40g carbohydrate, 12g fiber, 3g sugars, 17g protein.

Stefanie Schmidt, *Las Vegas, NV*

Grandma's Zucchini Bread

Growing up, my favorite harvest memory was going over to Grandma's house to pick zucchini and make her delicious bread.

Makes 2 loaves, serves 16

3 c. all-purpose flour
1 t. salt
¼ t. baking powder
1 t. baking soda
1 T. ground cinnamon
3 eggs, beaten
1 c. oil
2 t. vanilla extract
2¼ c. sugar
2 zucchini, shredded
½ c. chopped walnuts

Sift flour, salt, baking powder, baking soda and cinnamon together; set aside. Beat eggs, oil, vanilla and sugar together; add to flour mixture and blend well. Stir in zucchini and nuts until well combined. Pour batter into 2 lightly oiled 8"x4" loaf pans. Bake at 325 degrees for 40 to 60 minutes. Cool in pans on a wire rack for 20 minutes. Remove from pans and let cool.

Nutrition Per Serving: 356 calories, 17g fat, 2g sat fat, 35mg cholesterol, 242mg sodium, 47g carbohydrate, 1g fiber, 29g sugars, 4g protein.

Grandma's Zucchini Bread

Kathie Poritz, *Burlington, WI*

Kathie's Beef & Barley Soup

I make this soup ahead to have ready for the end of a shopping day. My daughters and I put our feet up and rest. When we're ready to eat, all I have to do is reheat the soup!

Serves 8

1 lb. beef shank
1/4 c. celery, diced
2 T. fresh parsley, chopped
1/2 t. salt
2 t. Worcestershire sauce
1 bay leaf
1/4 t. dried thyme
8 c. water
1/2 c. pearled barley
1 c. turnip, peeled and diced
1 c. carrots, peeled and sliced
1/2 c. onion, chopped

In a large stockpot over medium-high heat, combine beef, celery, parsley, salt, sauce, bay leaf, thyme and water. Cover and bring to a boil; reduce heat and simmer 2 hours. Remove beef from broth. When cool enough to handle, cut off meat and dice into bite-size pieces; set aside. Strain broth and return to stockpot; stir in barley and simmer, covered, about 30 minutes. Add remaining vegetables and beef; simmer until vegetables are tender, about 30 minutes. Discard bay leaf before serving.

Nutrition Per Serving: 133 calories, 2g fat, 1g sat fat, 22mg cholesterol, 149mg sodium, 14g carbohydrate, 3g fiber, 2g sugars, 14g protein.

Lisa Sett, *Thousand Oaks, CA*

Slow-Cooker Chile Verde Soup

Just the right combination of spices makes this an all-time favorite!

Serves 8

1/2 lb. pork tenderloin, cut into 1/2-inch cubes
1 t. oil
2 c. low-sodium chicken broth
2 15-oz. cans low-sodium white beans, drained and rinsed
2 4-oz. cans diced green chiles
1/4 t. ground cumin
1/4 t. dried oregano
salt and pepper to taste
Optional: chopped fresh cilantro

Cook pork in oil in a skillet over medium heat for one to 2 minutes, until browned. Place pork in a 4-quart slow cooker. Add remaining ingredients except cilantro; stir well. Cover and cook on low setting for 4 to 6 hours. Sprinkle cilantro over each serving, if desired.

Nutrition Per Serving: 151 calories, 2g fat, 0g sat fat, 14mg cholesterol, 568mg sodium, 21g carbohydrate, 8g fiber, 0g sugars, 13g protein.

Kitchen Helper

When you find you have leftover soup, ladle 2-cup portions into freezer bags...seal, label and freeze. Just reheat when you need a quick-fix meal.

Slow-Cooker Chili Verde Soup

Chapter Five

Dressed for Dinner

Set the table in style and get ready for some **Healthy, Happy & Homemade Dishes** that are sure to please. Show off your talents in the kitchen by making Cilantro Chicken Skillet and serving it in homemade Tortilla Bowls. How impressive! Chock-full of tasty veggies, Beef & Snap Pea Stir-Fry is a winner! In the mood for a little comfort food? Our favorite Scalloped Potatoes with Ham fills the bill and fills you up! It is time for dinner and you are ready with the perfect recipes...good-for-you!

Audrey Lett, *Newark, DE*

Gran's Rosemary Roast Chicken

Tuck some tiny new potatoes and baby carrots around this yummy chicken!

Serves 6

4-lb. roasting chicken
$1/2$ t. salt
$1/4$ t. pepper
1 onion, quartered
4 cloves garlic, pressed
$1/4$ c. fresh rosemary, chopped
2 T. butter, melted

Place chicken in a greased large roasting pan; sprinkle with salt and pepper. Place onion, garlic and rosemary inside chicken; brush butter over chicken. Bake, uncovered, at 400 degrees for $1^1/2$ hours, basting with pan juices, until golden and juices run clear when chicken is pierced with a fork.

Nutrition Per Serving: 179 calories, 7g fat, 3g sat fat, 87mg cholesterol, 283mg sodium, 3g carbohydrate, 1g fiber, 1g sugars, 24g protein.

Sandra Sullivan, *Aurora, CO*

Beef & Snap Pea Stir-Fry

In a rush? Spice up tonight's dinner with my go-to recipe for healthy in a hurry! Substitute chicken or pork for the beef, if you like.

Makes 4 servings

1 c. brown rice, uncooked
1 lb. beef sirloin steak, thinly sliced
1 T. cornstarch
$1/4$ t. salt
$1/4$ t. pepper
2 t. canola oil
$3/4$ c. water
1 lb. sugar snap peas, trimmed and halved
1 red pepper, cut into bite-size pieces
6 green onions, thinly sliced diagonally, white and green parts divided
1 T. fresh ginger, peeled and grated
$1/2$ t. red pepper flakes
salt and pepper to taste
2 T. lime juice

Cook rice according to package directions. Fluff with a fork; cover and set aside. Meanwhile, sprinkle beef with cornstarch, salt and pepper; toss to coat. Heat oil in a skillet over medium-high heat. Add half of beef and brown on both sides. Transfer to a plate; repeat with remaining beef. Stir in water, peas, red pepper, white part of onions, ginger and red pepper flakes; season with salt and pepper. Cook until peas turn bright green, one to 2 minutes. Return beef to skillet; cook for another 2 to 3 minutes. Remove from heat. Stir in lime juice and green part of onions. Serve over rice.

Nutrition Per Serving: 495 calories, 18g fat, 6g sat fat, 85mg cholesterol, 220mg sodium, 51g carbohydrate, 6g fiber, 6g sugars, 31g protein.

Beef & Snap Pea Stir-Fry

Cathy Webster, *Poughkeepsie, NY*

Scalloped Potatoes with Ham

This is one of our favorite comfort food recipes. We make it often!

Serves 8

1 onion, chopped
1 T. oil
3 cloves garlic, finely chopped
2 sweet potatoes, peeled and cut into ¼-inch slices
2 potatoes, peeled and cut into ¼-inch slices
½ c. all-purpose flour
1 t. salt
¼ t. pepper
2 c. cooked ham, chopped
1½ c. shredded Gruyère cheese, divided
1¾ c. 2% milk
1 T. butter, cut into pieces

Sauté onion in oil in a saucepan over medium-high heat 5 minutes, or until tender. Add garlic; cook 30 seconds. Remove from heat and set aside. Place potatoes in a large bowl. Combine flour, salt and pepper; sprinkle over potatoes, tossing to coat. Arrange half of potato mixture in a greased 13"x9" baking pan or 3-quart gratin dish. Top with onion, ham and one cup cheese. Top with remaining potato mixture. Pour milk over potato mixture. Dot with butter; cover with aluminum foil. Bake at 400 degrees for 50 minutes. Uncover, top with remaining ½ cup cheese and bake 20 more minutes, or until potatoes are tender and cheese is golden. Let stand 10 minutes before serving.

Nutrition Per Serving: 288 calories, 12g fat, 6g sat fat, 38mg cholesterol, 817mg sodium, 29g carbohydrate, 3g fiber, 5g sugars, 17g protein.

Kelly Patrick, *Ashburn, VA*

Summer Squash Pie

My mother and I have used this recipe every summer when summer squash is abundant.

Makes 6 to 8 servings

3 c. yellow squash, peeled and diced
½ c. onion, chopped
4 eggs, beaten
⅓ c. canola oil
1 c. biscuit baking mix
½ c. shredded part-skim mozzarella cheese
¼ t. pepper

Mix all ingredients in a bowl. Pat into a 9" pie plate lightly coated with non-stick vegetable spray. Bake at 350 degrees for 50 minutes to one hour, until set. Let stand for 10 minutes; slice into wedges. Serve warm or cold.

Nutrition Per Serving: 288 calories, 20g fat, 5g sat fat, 130mg cholesterol, 386mg sodium, 17g carbohydrate, 1g fiber, 5g sugars, 9g protein.

Kerry Mayer, *Dunham Springs, LA*

Creole Beef & Noodles

This dish tastes like it took a lot of effort, but stirs up in a jiffy! The night before, I move the beef from the freezer into the fridge. In the morning, it slices so easily when partly frozen.

Makes 4 servings

³/₄ lb. beef round steak, sliced into thin strips
1 green pepper, chopped
1 onion, chopped
1 tomato, chopped
1 clove garlic, pressed
1 t. dried parsley
¹/₄ t. salt
¹/₈ t. pepper
¹/₂ c. low-sodium beef broth
2 T. cornstarch
2 T. cold water
2 c. cooked wide egg noodles

Combine beef, vegetables, garlic and seasonings in a slow cooker. Drizzle with beef broth. Cover and cook on low setting for 7 to 8 hours, until beef is tender. Shortly before serving time, dissolve cornstarch in cold water; stir into slow cooker. Turn to high setting. Cover and cook for about 10 minutes, until slightly thickened. To serve, spoon beef mixture over cooked noodles.

Nutrition Per Serving: 260 calories, 5g fat, 1g sat fat, 74mg cholesterol, 251mg sodium, 30g carbohydrate, 2g fiber, 4g sugars, 25g protein.

Michelle Waddington, *New Bedford, MA*

Baked Crumbed Haddock

Delicious! Serve with mac & cheese and steamed broccoli for a down-home dinner.

Serves 8

2 5¹/₂-oz. pkgs. onion & garlic croutons
¹/₄ c. butter, melted
3 lbs. haddock fillets
Optional: lemon slices

Finely grind croutons in a food processor. Toss together croutons and butter. Place fish in a lightly greased 13"x9" baking pan. Sprinkle crouton mixture over fish. Bake, uncovered, at 350 degrees for 20 to 25 minutes, until fish flakes easily with a fork. Top fish with lemon slices, if desired.

Nutrition Per Serving: 358 calories, 14g fat, 6g sat fat, 110mg cholesterol, 788mg sodium, 25g carbohydrate, 2g fiber, 2g sugars, 32g protein.

Chicken Cacciatore

Wendi Knowles, *Pittsfield, ME*

Chicken Cacciatore

We love this classic chicken recipe! Make plenty because it warms up well.

Makes 10 servings

3 lbs. chicken, skin removed
1/4 c. all-purpose flour
1 T. olive oil
1 c. onion, thinly sliced
1/2 c. green pepper, sliced
1 clove garlic, minced
1/4 c. unsalted chicken broth
15-oz. can no-salt diced tomatoes, drained
8-oz. can no-salt tomato sauce
1/4 c. sliced mushrooms
1/4 t. dried oregano
1/8 t. salt

Pat chicken pieces dry; coat with flour. In a large skillet, heat oil over medium heat. Place chicken in skillet and cook for 15 to 20 minutes, until golden on both sides. Remove chicken to a plate; cover with aluminum foil and set aside. Add onion, green pepper and garlic to drippings in skillet; cook and stir until vegetables are tender. Add broth, scraping up brown bits in bottom of skillet. Add remaining ingredients; stir until blended. Return chicken to skillet, spooning some of the sauce over chicken. Cover and cook for about one hour, until chicken is tender and juices run clear.

Nutrition Per Serving: 158 calories, 4g fat, 1g sat fat, 62mg cholesterol, 226mg sodium, 8g carbohydrate, 2g fiber, 3g sugars, 21g protein.

Kelli Venable, *Ostrander, OH*

Fresh Veggies & Angel Hair

My mom & I love this yummy summertime meal...just add a slice or two of garlic bread and enjoy!

Makes 2 servings

7-oz. pkg. angel hair pasta, uncooked
1 T. olive oil
2 zucchini, peeled if desired and diced
2 yellow squash, diced
1 c. sliced mushrooms
1/2 c. onion, chopped
salt and pepper to taste

Divide pasta in half; reserve one-half for another recipe. Cook remaining pasta according to package directions; drain. Meanwhile, heat oil in a skillet over medium heat. Add zucchini, yellow squash, mushrooms and onion to skillet; cook until crisp-tender. Season with salt and pepper; ladle sauce over pasta.

Nutrition Per Serving: 458 calories, 9g fat, 1g sat fat, 0mg cholesterol, 10mg sodium, 80g carbohydrate, 4g fiber, 5g sugars, 15g protein.

Kitchen Helper

Chop up veggies like zucchini and yellow squash ahead of time and keep in a sealed plastic bag until ready to use later in the day. Add a few drops of lemon juice to keep the color fresh.

Kristin Stone, *Little Elm, TX*

Basil Chicken & Tortellini

This scrumptious dish evolved from a recipe my mother used to make. We love it...I hope your family will too!

Makes 6 servings

2¹/₂ c. cheese tortellini, uncooked
14-oz. pkg. frozen broccoli flowerets
3 boneless, skinless chicken breasts, cubed
1 t. garlic, minced
¹/₂ c. basil pesto sauce
¹/₄ c. low-sodium chicken broth
2 T. lemon juice
2 T. water
1 T. plus 2 t. fresh basil, chopped
Optional: fresh basil sprigs

Cook pasta according to package directions, adding broccoli along with pasta; drain. Meanwhile, spray a large non-stick skillet with non-stick vegetable spray. Over medium-high heat, cook chicken with garlic for about 2 minutes, until chicken is golden on all sides. Add remaining ingredients except basil sprigs to skillet, stirring to mix. Reduce heat to medium-low. Cover and simmer for 6 to 8 minutes, stirring occasionally, until chicken juices run clear. To serve, spoon chicken mixture over pasta and broccoli. Garnish with basil sprigs, if desired.

Nutrition Per Serving: 378 calories, 22g fat, 5g sat fat, 59mg cholesterol, 359mg sodium, 25g carbohydrate, 2g fiber, 1g sugars, 22g protein.

Michelle Powell, *Valley, AL*

Comforting Creamed Corn

We love this recipe when we are in the mood for some real comfort food!

Makes 8 servings

1 T. butter
4 c. corn, thawed if frozen
¹/₂ c. plain Greek yogurt
2 T. grated Parmesan cheese
1 t. dried basil

Melt butter in a non-stick skillet over medium heat; add corn. Cook for about 6 minutes, stirring occasionally, until tender. Reduce heat; stir in yogurt and cook for 4 minutes. Stir in cheese and basil just before serving.

Nutrition Per Serving: 88 calories, 2g fat, 1g sat fat, 6mg cholesterol, 39mg sodium, 15g carbohydrate, 1g fiber, 2g sugars, 4g protein.

Stacie Avner, *Delaware, OH*

Dijon Chicken & Fresh Herbs

I love making this family favorite in the summertime with my fresh garden herbs.

Serves 6

6 boneless, skinless chicken breasts
1/2 t. kosher salt
1 t. pepper
3 to 4 T. Dijon mustard
2 T. fresh rosemary, minced
2 T. fresh thyme, minced
2 T. fresh parsley, minced

Sprinkle chicken with salt and pepper. Grill over medium-high heat 6 minutes per side, or until juices run clear. Remove from grill and brush both sides with mustard; sprinkle with herbs.

Nutrition Per Serving: 283 calories, 6g fat, 1g sat fat, 172mg cholesterol, 303mg sodium, 0g carbohydrate, 0g fiber, 0g sugars, 53g protein.

Tara Horton, *Delaware, OH*

Black Bean & Rice Enchiladas

Using fresh cilantro in this recipe is the best!

Makes 8 servings

1 green pepper, chopped
1/4 c. onion, chopped
3 cloves garlic, minced
1 T. olive oil

15-oz. can black beans, drained and rinsed
14 1/4-oz. can diced tomatoes with green chiles
1/4 c. taco sauce
1 T. chili powder
1 t. ground cumin
1/4 t. red pepper flakes
2 c. cooked brown rice
8 10-inch multi-grain flour tortillas
1 c. salsa
1/2 c. shredded low-fat Cheddar cheese
3 T. fresh cilantro, chopped

In a skillet over medium heat, sauté green pepper, onion and garlic in oil until tender. Add beans, tomatoes, taco sauce and seasonings. Simmer until heated through and mixture thickens. Add rice; cook 5 minutes. Spoon filling down the center of each tortilla. Roll up tortillas; place in a lightly greased 13"x9" baking pan. Spoon salsa over tortillas. Bake, covered, at 350 degrees for 25 minutes. Uncover; sprinkle with cheese and cilantro. Bake an additional 3 minutes, until cheese is melted.

Nutrition Per Serving: 262 calories, 4g fat, 1g sat fat, 5mg cholesterol, 766mg sodium, 48g carbohydrate, 10g fiber, 4g sugars, 14g protein.

Debra Van Zant, *Stevenson Ranch, CA*

Basil & Tomato Halibut

Slices of garden-fresh tomatoes and a sprinkle of freshly chopped basil taste amazing spooned over servings of fish.

Makes 6 servings

1 onion, sliced
4 cloves garlic, minced
1 T. olive oil
1 t. butter
8 roma tomatoes, diced
14½-oz. can low-sodium chicken broth
1 t. seafood seasoning
¼ t. pepper
2 lbs. halibut fillets
cooked rice
fresh basil to taste, chopped

In a skillet over medium heat, sauté onion and garlic in oil and butter for 3 minutes. Stir in tomatoes, broth and seasonings. Add fish to skillet. Cook, covered, over medium heat until fish flakes easily, about 8 minutes. Remove fish from sauce and lay on a bed of rice. Add basil to sauce; stir and spoon over fish and rice.

Nutrition Per Serving: 441 calories, 6g fat, 1g sat fat, 76mg cholesterol, 227mg sodium, 60g carbohydrate, 1g fiber, 3g sugars, 35g protein.

Jen Sell, *Farmington, MN*

Chicken Cordon Bleu

A special dish I serve family & friends. It is delicious and beautiful every time.

Makes 4 servings

4 4-oz. boneless, skinless chicken breasts
2 slices deli low-sodium ham, cut in half
2 slices reduced-fat Swiss cheese, cut in half
1 egg, beaten
½ c. skim milk
¼ c. whole-grain bread crumbs
½ t. garlic powder
1 t. dried oregano
2 T. grated Parmesan cheese

Flatten chicken breasts between 2 pieces of wax paper until ¼-inch thick. Top each piece with a ½ slice of ham and cheese; roll up tightly, securing with toothpicks. In a small bowl, beat egg and milk together; set aside. In another bowl, combine bread crumbs, garlic powder, oregano and Parmesan cheese. Dip each chicken bundle in egg mixture, then in bread crumbs. Place on a greased baking sheet; bake at 350 degrees for 45 minutes.

Nutrition Per Serving: 236 calories, 6g fat, 2g sat fat, 126mg cholesterol, 352mg sodium, 8g carbohydrate, 1g fiber, 2g sugars, 36g protein.

Chicken Cordon Bleu

Grecia Williams, *Scottsville, KY*

Chicken Kiev

This classic recipe is always a favorite for special occasions or when you just want to serve your family something extra yummy!

Serves 8

1½ c. dry bread crumbs
½ c. shredded Parmesan cheese
1 t. dried basil
1 t. dried oregano
½ t. garlic salt
½ t. salt
⅓ c. butter, melted and divided
1½ lbs. chicken tenders, about 8 tenders
¼ c. low-sodium chicken broth
¼ c. green onions, chopped
¼ c. dried parsley

Combine bread crumbs, cheese and seasonings in a large bowl. Reserve 3 tablespoons butter. Dip chicken in remaining melted butter. Dredge chicken in crumb mixture. Arrange chicken in a lightly greased 13"x9" baking pan. Bake, covered, at 375 degrees for 30 to 40 minutes, until chicken is tender. Heat broth, green onions, parsley and reserved butter in a small saucepan over medium heat until heated through. Spoon mixture over chicken and bake, covered, for 5 to 7 more minutes.

Nutrition Per Serving: 267 calories, 12g fat, 6g sat fat, 72mg cholesterol, 579mg sodium, 16g carbohydrate, 1g fiber, 1g sugars, 24g protein.

Tara Horton, *Delaware, OH*

Chicken Pesto Primo

One summer I grew basil in my garden and froze batches of homemade pesto in ice cube trays. I made up this recipe to use that yummy pesto. When asparagus isn't in season, I'll toss in some broccoli flowerets...it's just as tasty!

Makes 4 servings

8-oz. pkg. rotini pasta, cooked
2 c. cooked chicken, cubed
1 c. asparagus, steamed and cut into 1-inch pieces
2 T. basil pesto sauce
¼ to ½ c. chicken broth

Cook pasta according to package directions; drain. In a skillet over medium heat, combine chicken, asparagus, pesto, cooked pasta and ¼ cup chicken broth. Cook and stir until heated through, adding more broth as needed.

Nutrition Per Serving: 268 calories, 9g fat, 2g sat fat, 61mg cholesterol, 125mg sodium, 19g carbohydrate, 2g fiber, 1g sugars, 27g protein.

Chicken Pesto Primo

Firecracker Grilled Salmon

Sharon Demers, *Dolores, CO*

Firecracker Grilled Salmon

We love making this spicy salmon on the grill and serve it with fresh green beans and quinoa. It is a favorite summer meal.

Makes 4 servings

4 4-oz. salmon fillets
1 t. sesame oil
1 T. low-sodium soy sauce
2 T. balsamic vinegar
2 T. green onions, chopped
1 t. brown sugar, packed
1 clove garlic, minced
1/2 t. red pepper flakes
1/2 t. sesame oil
1/8 t. salt

Place salmon in a casserole dish. Whisk together remaining ingredients and pour over salmon. Cover with plastic wrap; refrigerate 4 to 6 hours. Remove salmon, discarding marinade. Place on an aluminum foil-lined grill that has been sprayed with non-stick vegetable spray. Grill 10 minutes per inch of thickness, measured at thickest part, until fish flakes easily with a fork. Turn halfway through cooking.

Nutrition Per Serving: 214 calories, 10g fat, 2g sat fat, 58mg cholesterol, 175mg sodium, 5g carbohydrate, 0g fiber, 5g sugars, 24g protein

Melody Taynor, *Everett, WA*

Asian Country-Style Ribs

For a super-easy side, steam a package of frozen stir-fry veggies...top with crunchy chow mein noodles. Dinner is served!

Serves 8

4 lbs. boneless country-style pork ribs
1/4 c. brown sugar, packed
1 c. low-sodium soy sauce
1/4 c. sesame oil
2 T. olive oil
2 T. rice vinegar
2 T. lime juice
2 T. garlic, minced
2 T. fresh ginger, peeled and grated
1 t. hot pepper sauce
cooked brown rice

Place ribs in a large plastic zipping bag. Stir together remaining ingredients except rice; pour over ribs. Seal bag and refrigerate for 8 hours to overnight, turning bag occasionally to coat ribs with marinade. Drain marinade and discard; place ribs in a slow cooker. Cover and cook on low setting for 8 to 9 hours, until tender. Drain; shred ribs using 2 forks. Serve over cooked rice.

Nutrition Per Serving: 458 calories, 29g fat, 6g sat fat, 168mg cholesterol, 356 mg sodium, 3g carbohydrate, 0g fiber, 1g sugars, 44g protein

Country Veggie Bake

Pat Griedl, *Appleton, WI*

Country Veggie Bake

An easy dinner to toss together, then just pop it in the oven.

Makes 8 servings

1 T. olive oil
2 carrots, peeled, halved lengthwise and sliced
2 onions, chopped
1 to 2 cloves garlic, chopped
1 c. mushrooms, quartered
15-oz. can black beans, drained and rinsed
14-oz. can low-sodium vegetable or chicken
    broth
1 c. frozen corn
1/2 c. pearled barley, uncooked
1/4 c. bulghur wheat, uncooked
1/3 c. fresh parsley, snipped
dried thyme to taste
1/2 c. shredded low-fat Cheddar cheese

Heat oil in a large skillet over medium heat. Sauté carrots and onions until carrots are tender. Stir in garlic and mushrooms; sauté 3 minutes. Combine mixture with remaining ingredients except cheese. Spoon into a greased 2-quart casserole dish. Bake, covered, at 350 degrees for one hour, stirring once halfway through baking time. Top with cheese. Cover and let stand 5 minutes, or until cheese melts.

Nutrition Per Serving: 185 calories, 4g fat, 1g sat fat, 4mg cholesterol, 285mg sodium, 31g carbohydrate, 8g fiber, 3g sugars, 9g protein.

Robin Hill, *Rochester, NY,*

Braised Pork & Peppers

This savory dinner goes together in no time at all, and the colorful peppers look so festive.

Makes 4 servings

4 thick center-cut pork chops
1/4 t. salt
1/4 t. pepper
2 t. olive oil
1 T. tomato paste
1/2 c. onion, thinly sliced
1 yellow pepper, thinly sliced
1 red pepper, thinly sliced
4 cloves garlic, thinly sliced
1/2 t. dried thyme
1/2 c. low-sodium chicken broth

Season pork chops with salt and pepper. Heat oil in a large skillet over medium heat. Brown chops on both sides, about 6 to 8 minutes total. Remove to a plate and set aside. Add tomato paste to drippings in skillet; cook and stir for 15 seconds. Add onion and peppers. Cook, stirring occasionally, until almost tender, about 3 minutes. Add garlic; cook and stir for one minute. Add thyme and broth. Bring to a boil, scraping up browned bits in bottom of skillet. Return chops to skillet; reduce heat to medium-low. Cover and cook about 4 minutes; turn chops over. Cover and cook chops another 3 to 5 minutes, until chops are cooked through. Serve chops topped with vegetable mixture.

Nutrition Per Serving: 334 calories, 18g fat, 6g sat fat, 92mg cholesterol, 247mg sodium, 8g carbohydrate, 1g fiber, 4g sugars, 34g protein.

Irene Robinson, *Cincinnati, OH*

Lemony Broccoli

A tang of lemon with fresh broccoli...a winning combination.

Makes 6 servings

1½ lbs. broccoli, cut into spears
½ clove garlic, minced
2 T. olive oil
2 T. lemon juice

Add broccoli to a saucepan with a small amount of water. Over medium-high heat, cook broccoli 6 to 8 minutes, until crisp-tender. Drain. Sauté garlic in oil over medium heat, until tender. Add lemon juice; mix well. Pour over broccoli, tossing gently to blend.

Nutrition Per Serving: 59 calories, 3g fat, 0g sat fat, 0mg cholesterol, 38mg sodium, 8g carbohydrate, 3g fiber, 2g sugars, 3g protein.

Christian Brown, *Killeen, TX*

Deep South Chicken & Dumplings

This delicious comfort food is our family favorite. I serve it with a fruit salad...perfect!

Serves 8

4-lb. roasting chicken
Supreme Sauce
Dumplings
salt and pepper to taste
Garnish: fresh parsley

Bake chicken, covered, in an ungreased roasting pan at 350 degrees for 1½ hours. Let chicken cool while preparing Supreme Sauce. Shred chicken; add to simmering sauce in Dutch oven. Drop Dumplings into sauce by heaping tablespoonfuls. Cover and cook over high heat 10 to 15 minutes, until dumplings are firm and puffy. Discard bay leaves. Add salt and pepper; garnish with fresh parsley.

SUPREME SAUCE:

2 T. butter
1 T. oil
½ c. carrot, peeled and diced
½ c. celery, diced
3 cloves garlic, minced
2 bay leaves
5 T. all-purpose flour
6 c. low-sodium chicken broth
¼ c. 2% milk

Melt butter and oil in a Dutch oven over medium heat. Add vegetables, garlic and bay leaves. Sauté until soft. Stir in flour; add broth, one cup at a time, stirring well after each addition. Simmer until thickened; stir in milk.

DUMPLINGS:

2 c. all-purpose flour
1 T. baking powder
1 t. salt
2 eggs
¾ to 1 c. buttermilk, divided

Mix flour, baking powder and salt. Whisk together eggs and ¾ cup buttermilk; fold into flour mixture. Stir just until dough forms, adding a little more buttermilk if needed.

Nutrition Per Serving: 732 calories, 44g fat, 13g sat fat, 222mg cholesterol, 595mg sodium, 34g carbohydrate, 1g fiber, 3g sugars, 49g protein.

Deep South Chicken & Dumplings

Homemade Fish Sticks

Shelley Turner, *Boise, ID*

Homemade Fish Sticks

My kids love these yummy fish sticks! I serve them in diner-style baskets with French fries.

Makes 8 servings

2 lbs. cod fillets
2 eggs
2 T. water
salt and pepper to taste
1½ c. seasoned dry bread crumbs
3 T. grated Parmesan cheese
¼ c. olive oil
½ c. tartar sauce
Optional: lemon wedges

Cut fish into 4-inch by one-inch strips; set aside. In a shallow dish, beat together egg, water and seasonings. In a separate dish, mix bread crumbs and cheese. Dip fish into egg mixture; coat with bread crumb mixture and set aside. Heat olive oil in a skillet over medium-high heat. Working in batches, add fish to skillet and cook until flaky and golden, about 3 minutes per side. Drain fish sticks on paper towels. Serve with lemon wedges, if desired.

Nutrition Per Serving: 298 calories, 13g fat, 3g sat fat, 99mg cholesterol, 516mg sodium, 18g carbohydrate, 1g fiber, 2g sugars, 26g protein.

Amy Butcher, *Columbus, GA*

Garlicky Baked Shrimp

Here's the perfect party recipe...guests peel their own shrimp and save you the work!

Serves 6

2 lbs. uncooked large shrimp, cleaned and
  unpeeled
16-oz. bottle light Italian salad dressing
1½ T. pepper
2 cloves garlic, pressed
2 lemons, halved
¼ c. fresh parsley, chopped
2 T. butter, cut into small pieces

Place shrimp, salad dressing, pepper and garlic in an ungreased 13"x9" baking pan, tossing to coat. Squeeze juice from lemons over shrimp mixture; stir. Cut lemon halves into wedges and add to pan. Sprinkle shrimp with parsley; dot with butter. Bake, uncovered, at 375 degrees for 25 minutes, stirring after 15 minutes. Serve in pan.

Nutrition Per Serving: 224 calories, 13g fat, 4g sat fat, 201mg cholesterol, 1370mg sodium, 8g carbohydrate, 2g fiber, 1g sugars, 21g protein.

Good & Healthy "Fried" Chicken

Cris Goode, *Morresville, IN*

Good & Healthy "Fried" Chicken

We love this healthier version of everyone's favorite food...fried chicken!

Makes 5 servings

1 c. whole-grain panko bread crumbs
1 c. cornmeal
2 T. all-purpose flour
salt and pepper to taste
1 c. buttermilk
10 chicken drumsticks

Combine panko, cornmeal, flour, salt and pepper in a gallon-size plastic zipping bag. Coat chicken with buttermilk, one piece at a time. Drop chicken into bag and shake to coat pieces lightly. Arrange chicken on a baking pan coated with non-stick vegetable spray. Bake, uncovered, at 350 degrees for 40 to 50 minutes, until chicken juices run clear.

Nutrition Per Serving: 285 calories, 8g fat, 2g sat fat, 69mg cholesterol, 147mg sodium, 32g carbohydrate, 1g fiber, 3g sugars, 21g protein.

> ### ∼ **Healthy Fact** ∼
> The dark meat of the chicken has a few more calories than the white meat, but it contains more iron, zinc, riboflavin, thiamine, and vitamins B6 and B12. Whatever you choose, it has less fat than most cuts of red meat.

Diana Migliaccio, *Clifton, NJ*

Captain's Favorite Tilapia

I like to serve rice pilaf and spinach salad alongside this flavorful fish dish.

Makes 4 servings

¼ c. olive oil
1 sweet onion, thinly sliced
1 lb. tilapia fillets
12 Kalamata olives, chopped
8 cloves garlic, chopped
¼ c. fresh basil, chopped, or 1 T. dried basil
2 tomatoes, thinly sliced
salt and pepper to taste
Optional: lemon wedges

Heat olive oil in an oven-proof skillet over medium heat. Sauté onion slices for 3 minutes per side, or until translucent. Arrange fish over onion; sprinkle with olives, garlic and basil. Place tomato slices on top. Add salt and pepper to taste. Remove skillet to center oven rack. Bake, uncovered, at 375 degrees for 12 to 15 minutes, until fish flakes easily with a fork. Garnish with lemon wedges, if desired.

Nutrition Per Serving: 275 calories, 17g fat, 3g sat fat, 57mg cholesterol, 162mg sodium, 8g carbohydrate, 2g fiber, 3g sugars, 24g protein.

Sandy Coffey, *Cincinnati, OH*

Slow-Cooked Creamy Potatoes

Everytime I make this comforting recipe I get compliments! The secret to the creaminess is the cream cheese. Everyone always wants this special recipe!

Serves 6

4 green onions, chopped
2 cloves garlic, minced
8 potatoes, sliced and divided
½ t. salt, divided
¼ t. pepper, divided
8-oz. pkg. low-fat cream cheese, diced and divided

Combine green onions and garlic in a small bowl; set aside. Layer one-quarter of the potato slices in a greased slow cooker; sprinkle with half of the salt and pepper. Top with one-third each of cream cheese and green onion mixture. Repeat layers twice, ending with potatoes; sprinkle with remaining salt and pepper. Cover and cook on high setting for 3 hours. Stir to blend melted cheese; cover and cook for an additional hour. Stir well and mash slightly before serving.

Nutrition Per Serving: 259 calories, 6g fat, 4g sat fat, 20mg cholesterol, 402mg sodium, 44g carbohydrate, 5g fiber, 4g sugars, 8g protein.

Jennifer Martineau, *Delaware, OH*

Gramma's Smothered Swiss Steak

This classic recipe is perfect for any night of the week, but I often serve it for Sunday lunch. I serve it with fresh green beans and roasted potatoes....what a treat!

Serves 6

1½ lbs. beef round steak, cut into serving-size pieces
1 T. oil
1 small onion, halved and sliced
1 carrot, peeled and shredded
1 c. sliced mushrooms
10¾-oz. can low-sodium cream of chicken soup
8-oz. can no-salt tomato sauce

Brown beef in oil in a skillet over medium heat; drain and set aside. Arrange vegetables in a slow cooker; place beef on top. Mix together soup and tomato sauce; pour over beef and vegetables. Cover and cook on low setting for 6 hours, or until beef is tender.

Nutrition Per Serving: 381 calories, 20g fat, 8g sat fat, 111mg cholesterol, 237mg sodium, 10g carbohydrate, 1g fiber, 3g sugars, 36g protein.

Gramma's Smothered Swiss Steak

Grilled Market Veggies

Regina Wickline, *Pebble Beach, CA*

Grilled Market Veggies

Your friends will be impressed when it is your turn to grill next time when you serve this beautiful and easy veggie dish!

Makes 6 servings

3 zucchini, sliced ¾-inch thick
3 yellow squash, sliced ¾-inch thick
1 baby eggplant, sliced ¾-inch thick
1 sweet onion, sliced ¾-inch thick
2 tomatoes, sliced 1-inch thick
½ c. balsamic vinegar
⅛ c. canola oil
2 cloves garlic, minced
1 T. fresh rosemary, minced
1 T. fresh oregano, chopped
1 T. fresh basil, chopped
1 T. fresh parsley, minced
1 t. sugar
¼ t. salt
¼ t. pepper

Combine vegetables in a large bowl. Whisk together remaining ingredients and pour over vegetables. Toss to coat. Marinate for 30 minutes to one hour. Remove vegetables from marinade with a slotted spoon. Arrange on a grill over medium-hot heat. Grill 2 to 5 minutes on each side, basting often with marinade, until tender.

Nutrition Per Serving: 123 calories, 5g fat, 1g sat fat, 0mg cholesterol, 121mg sodium, 17g carbohydrate, 5g fiber, 12g sugars, 3g protein.

Sonya Labbe, *West Hollywood, CA*

Vegetarian Mexican Pie

When we moved to Los Angeles, I started searching for Mexican dishes that my family would love. This recipe is one of them. It's easy to make, yet so much better than any fast food.

Makes 6 servings

12 6-inch corn tortillas
1 c. low-sodium black beans, drained
   and rinsed
1 c. low-sodium red kidney beans, drained
   and rinsed
4-oz. can chopped green chiles
1½ c. green or red salsa
1 c. plain Greek yogurt
1 c. shredded Monterey Jack cheese

Layer 4 of the tortillas in a lightly greased 8"x8" baking pan, overlapping slightly. Top tortillas with ½ cup black beans, ½ cup kidney beans, ¼ cup chiles, ½ cup salsa, ⅓ cup yogurt and ⅓ cup cheese. Add 4 more tortillas; repeat layering. Top with remaining tortillas, salsa, plain yogurt and cheese. Bake, uncovered, at 375 degrees, until bubbly and golden, 30 to 40 minutes.

Nutrition Per Serving: 285 calories, 8g fat, 4g sat fat, 19mg cholesterol, 940mg sodium, 40g carbohydrate, 10g fiber, 6g sugars, 16g protein.

Nancy Wise, *Little Rock, AR*

Homestyle Green Beans

This is such a tasty way to serve fresh green beans...perfect alongside a baked ham.

Serves 8

2 lbs. green beans, trimmed
2 c. water
1 t. salt, divided
1/3 c. butter
1 1/2 T. sugar
1 t. dried basil
1/2 t. garlic powder
1/4 t. pepper
2 c. cherry tomatoes, halved

Place beans in a Dutch oven; add water and 1/2 teaspoon salt. Bring to a boil over medium-high heat. Reduce heat to medium-low; cover and simmer for 15 minutes, or until tender. Drain beans; keep warm. Meanwhile, melt butter in a saucepan over medium heat. Stir in sugar, basil, garlic powder, remaining salt and pepper Add tomatoes and cook, stirring gently, until heated through. Spoon tomato mixture over warm beans and toss gently.

Nutrition Per Serving: 118 calories, 8g fat, 5g sat fat, 20mg cholesterol, 157mg sodium, 12g carbohydrate, 4g fiber, 7g sugars, 2g protein.

Rogene Rogers, *Bemidji, MN*

Kona Honey Chicken

A family favorite! To complete the tropical theme, stir some pineapple tidbits into your favorite creamy coleslaw.

Serves 10

3 lbs. chicken
1/2 c. green onions, chopped
1/2 c. low- sodium soy sauce
1/4 c. apple juice
1/2 c. water
1/2 c. honey

Place chicken pieces in a slow cooker. Mix together onions, sauce, juice and water; pour over chicken. Cover and cook on low setting for 3 to 5 hours, until chicken is tender. Remove chicken from slow cooker. Brush with honey and place on an ungreased broiler pan. Broil for a few minutes until golden, brushing with honey several times. Serve chicken with sauce from slow cooker.

Nutrition Per Serving: 226 calories, 4g fat, 1g sat fat, 99mg cholesterol, 487 mg sodium, 16g carbohydrate, 0g fiber, 15g sugars, 31g protein.

Place vegetables and garlic in bag; place roast in bag on top of vegetables. Drizzle broth mixture over roast; season with salt and pepper. Cut 6, one-inch holes in top of roasting bag with a knife tip. Seal bag. Bake at 325 degrees for 3 hours, or until roast is tender. Remove roast to a serving platter; let stand 15 minutes before slicing. Serve vegetables with roast.

Nutrition Per Serving: 484 calories, 33g fat, 13g sat fat, 166mg cholesterol, 285mg sodium, 8g carbohydrate, 2g fiber, 3g sugars, 37g protein.

Debbie Donaldson, *Andalusia, AL*

Mama's Scrumptious Roast Beef

Your family will love this flavorful beef roast!

Serves 10

14-oz. can low-sodium garlic-seasoned
  chicken broth
1 c. low-sodium chicken broth
3 T. red steak sauce
2 T. brown steak sauce
2 T. balsamic vinegar
1 T. all-purpose flour
14 baby carrots
2 red peppers, thinly sliced
2 bunches green onions, chopped
6 cloves garlic, minced
4-lb. beef rump roast
salt and pepper to taste

Combine first 5 ingredients in a large bowl; set aside. Place flour in a large plastic roasting bag; shake bag to coat and arrange in a roasting pan.

Lori Rosenberg, *University Heights, OH*

Pesto Polenta Lasagna

This vegetarian dish will please everyone!

Makes 8 servings

18-oz. tube polenta, sliced $1/4$-inch thick and
  divided
$1/4$ c. basil pesto sauce, divided
$1^{1}/4$ c. marinara sauce, divided
1 c. shredded part-skim mozzarella cheese
$1/4$ c. pine nuts

In a greased 11"x7" baking pan, arrange half of polenta slices in a single layer. Spread half of pesto over polenta; then spoon half of marinara. Repeat layering, ending with marinara sauce. Bake, uncovered, at 375 degrees for 25 minutes. Remove from oven; top with cheese and pine nuts. Place pan under a preheated broiler; broil until cheese is melted and nuts are toasted.

Nutrition Per Serving: 196 calories, 11g fat, 3g sat fat, 10mg cholesterol, 517mg sodium, 17g carbohydrate, 2g fiber, 2g sugars, 7g protein.

Susan Province, *Strawberry Plains, TN*

Susan's Vegetable Lasagna

I created this recipe for my family as a way to add more vegetables to our meals. It's really versatile...use any fresh veggies you like.

Serves 8

2 t. olive oil

6 c. vegetables, diced, such as zucchini, yellow squash, carrots, broccoli, red pepper, mushrooms

1 onion, diced

2 cloves garlic, minced

2 T. low-sodium soy sauce

1/4 t. pepper

1/2 t. dried basil

1/2 t. dried oregano

26-oz. jar marinara sauce, divided

9-oz. pkg. no-boil lasagna noodles, uncooked and divided

1 c. ricotta cheese

1 c. grated Parmesan cheese

1 c. shredded mozzarella cheese

Over medium-high heat, drizzle oil into a skillet. Add vegetables and onion; stir-fry until onion turns translucent. Add garlic and soy sauce; continue cooking until vegetables are tender. Season with pepper, basil and oregano. Spoon 1/2 cup sauce into an ungreased 13"x9" baking pan. Arrange 1/3 of the noodles on the bottom; spoon on half the ricotta cheese and half the Parmesan cheese. Top with half of the vegetables. Repeat again, ending with remaining noodles. Pour on the remaining sauce and sprinkle with mozzarella cheese. Bake, uncovered, at 350 degrees for 25 to 30 minutes.

Nutrition Per Serving: 251 calories, 14g fat, 7g sat fat, 45mg cholesterol, 802mg sodium, 17g carbohydrate, 3g fiber, 8g sugars, 15g protein.

Elizabeth Mullett, *Wilmington, MA*

Garden-Style Spaghetti

This flavorful dish can't be beat when the tomatoes are ripe and the herbs are fresh.

Makes 6 servings

16-oz. pkg. whole-wheat spaghetti, uncooked

2 lbs. ripe tomatoes, chopped

3 T. fresh basil, chopped

1 T. fresh rosemary, chopped

1 T. fresh thyme, chopped

1 T. fresh marjoram, chopped

1/2 c. olive oil

6 T. grated Parmesan cheese

Cook pasta according to package directions; drain. Meanwhile, place tomatoes and herbs in a large heat-proof serving bowl; set aside. Heat olive oil in a small saucepan over low heat until very hot. Carefully pour hot oil over tomato mixture; mix well. Add cooked pasta to tomato mixture and stir gently. Serve topped with grated cheese.

Nutrition Per Serving: 477 calories, 21g fat, 4g sat fat, 6mg cholesterol, 110mg sodium, 63g carbohydrate, 8g fiber, 4g sugars, 15g protein.

Garden-Style Spaghetti

Jo Ann, *Gooseberry Patch*

Meatloaf Mexicana

I like to serve this tasty dish alongside some zesty refried beans and a warm slice of cornbread. We also like to have a nice green salad with this rich meatloaf to round out the meal. So yummy!

Makes 8 servings

1 lb. ground pork
³/₄ lb. lean ground beef
1 c. shredded low-fat Monterey Jack cheese,
   divided
1 c. dry bread crumbs
¹/₂ c. taco sauce
2 eggs, beaten
1 T. fresh parsley, chopped
2 t. canned diced jalapeño peppers
Garnish: chopped tomatoes, sliced green
   onions

Combine meats, ³/₄ cup cheese and remaining ingredients except garnish in a large bowl. Gently press into a lightly greased 9"x5" loaf pan. Bake, uncovered at 350 degrees for 55 to 60 minutes, until no longer pink in center. Top with remaining cheese; garnish as desired.

Nutrition Per Serving: 302 calories, 16g fat, 6g sat fat, 116mg cholesterol, 448mg sodium, 12g carbohydrate, 1g fiber, 2g sugars, 26g protein.

Janet Bowlin, *Fayetteville, AR*

Country-Style Cabbage

Tossed with bacon and onion, this cabbage side is one tasty way to enjoy your daily dose of veggies!

Makes 6 servings

4 slices bacon, cut into ¹/₄-inch pieces
¹/₄ c. onion, thinly sliced
1 head cabbage, coarsely shredded
2 T. sugar
¹/₄ c. oil, divided
salt and pepper to taste

In a skillet over medium-high heat, cook bacon until crisp. Add onion and cook 2 minutes longer. Stir in cabbage and sugar. Add oil, one tablespoon at a time, as needed. Cook until cabbage begins to wilt, but is not completely soft. Serve immediately.

Nutrition Per Serving: 206 calories, 16g fat, 4g sat fat, 10mg cholesterol, 154mg sodium, 14g carbohydrate, 4g fiber, 9g sugars, 4g protein.

Elaine Lucas, *Runge, TX*

Mom's Spaghetti & Meatballs

Sometimes I like to serve this with whole-grain spaghetti and sometimes with spiralized zucchini...both are delicious!

Serves 6

2 8-oz. cans no-salt tomato sauce
½ t. garlic powder
½ t. dried oregano
½ t. dried basil
salt and pepper to taste
Meatballs
16-oz. pkg. whole-wheat spaghetti, cooked, or
   blanched spiralized or shaved zucchini
Garnish: shredded Parmesan cheese

In a large skillet over medium-low heat, combine tomato sauce and seasonings. Bring to a simmer. Meanwhile, make Meatballs. Add uncooked meatballs to sauce. Simmer over medium-low heat for about 30 minutes, turning occasionally, until meatballs are no longer pink in the center. Serve sauce and meatballs over spaghetti or zucchini. Garnish with Parmesan cheese.

MEATBALLS:

1 lb. lean ground beef
3 T. shredded Parmesan cheese
2 eggs, beaten
1 slice white bread, crumbled
½ t. garlic salt

Combine all ingredients in a large bowl; mix well. Form into 2-inch balls.

Nutrition Per Serving with whole-wheat pasta:
512 calories, 20g fat, 3g sat fat, 124mg cholesterol, 367mg sodium, 59g carbohydrate, 9g fiber, 3g sugars, 29g protein.

Nutrition Per Serving with zucchini: 275 calories, 18g fat, 3g sat fat, 124mg cholesterol, 367mg sodium, 8g carbohydrate, 1g fiber, 5g sugars, 18 g protein.

Mom's Spaghetti & Meatballs

Roberta's Pepper Steak

Roberta Goll, *Chesterfield, MI*

Roberta's Pepper Steak

This beef dish is as beautiful as it is yummy. I like to serve it right from the cast-iron skillet.

Makes 8 servings

1¼ lbs. beef round steak, sliced into
   ½-inch strips
2 t. canola oil
2 cloves garlic, pressed and divided
2 green peppers, cut into thin strips
2 onions, coarsely chopped
8-oz. pkg. sliced mushrooms
½ t. salt
½ t. pepper
1 c. low-sodium beef broth

In a skillet over medium heat, brown steak strips with oil and half the garlic. Add peppers and onions; cook until tender. Stir in mushrooms, salt, pepper and remaining garlic. Stir in beef broth. Reduce heat to low and simmer for one hour. Add a little water if needed.

Nutrition Per Serving: 213 calories, 10g fat, 3g sat fat, 71mg cholesterol, 318mg sodium, 6g carbohydrate, 1g fiber, 3g sugars, 25g protein.

Susana Rodriguez, *Rialto, CA*

Chicken Mole Verde

This recipe reminds me of my grandmother, who has long since passed. She was a wonderful cook and this was one of her favorite recipes.

Makes 6 servings

3½ lbs. chicken, cut up
½ onion
3 cloves garlic, divided
1 T. chicken soup base
¼ t. salt
6 green tomatoes
½ green jalapeño pepper, seeds removed if
   desired
½ c. shelled pumpkin seeds
¼ c. fresh cilantro, chopped
6 c. cooked Mexican rice

Place chicken in a stockpot; cover with water. Add onion, 2 cloves garlic, soup base and salt. Cook over medium-low heat until tender, 45 minutes to one hour. Drain, reserving one cup broth; return chicken to pot. Meanwhile, in a saucepan, cover tomatoes, jalapeño and remaining garlic clove with water. Cook over medium-high heat for 15 to 25 minutes, until tomatoes are soft and opaque green; drain. In a dry skillet over medium-high heat, toast pumpkin seeds until lightly golden, stirring often. Transfer tomato mixture, reserved broth, pumpkin seeds and cilantro into a blender. Process until smooth; add salt. Spoon tomato mixture over chicken. Cover; simmer over low heat until warmed through. Serve with favorite Mexican rice.

Nutrition Per Serving: 715 calories, 14g fat, 3g sat fat, 151mg cholesterol, 265mg sodium, 72g carbohydrate, 3g fiber, 8g sugars, 72g protein.

Rosemary Pork & Mushrooms

Vickie, *Gooseberry Patch*

Rosemary Pork & Mushrooms

This simple dish is delicious with ordinary button mushrooms, but for a special dinner I'll use a combination of wild mushrooms... their earthy flavor goes so well with the fresh rosemary.

Makes 4 servings, 2 slices each

1 lb. pork tenderloin, cut into 8 slices
1 T. butter
1 c. sliced mushrooms
2 T. onion, finely chopped
1 clove garlic, minced
1 t. fresh rosemary, chopped
1/4 t. celery salt
1 T. sherry or apple juice

Flatten each pork slice to one-inch thick; set aside. Melt butter in a large skillet over medium-high heat. Cook pork slices just until golden, about one minute per side. Remove pork slices to a plate, reserving drippings in skillet. Add remaining ingredients except sherry or apple juice to skillet. Reduce heat to low; cook for 2 minutes, stirring frequently. Stir in sherry or juice. Return pork slices to skillet; spoon mushroom mixture over top. Cover and simmer for 3 to 4 minutes, until the pork juices run clear. Serve pork slices topped with mushroom mixture.

Nutrition Per Serving: 249 calories, 10g fat, 4g sat fat, 114mg cholesterol, 222mg sodium, 2g carbohydrate, 1g fiber, 1g sugars, 35g protein.

Jen Stout, *Blandon, PA*

Spicy Roasted Potatoes

Mmm...potatoes seasoned with two kinds of mustard! This is a yummy, easy side dish. You don't even need to peel the potatoes.

Makes 4 servings

2 baking potatoes, cut into 1-inch cubes
1 1/2 t. dry mustard
1 1/2 t. Dijon mustard
1 t. olive oil
1 clove garlic, minced
1 T. fresh tarragon, chopped
1/4 t. paprika
1/8 t. cayenne pepper

Place potatoes in a bowl; set aside. In a separate bowl, combine remaining ingredients; stir well and pour over potatoes. Toss potatoes until well coated. Arrange potatoes in a single layer on a lightly greased baking sheet. Bake, uncovered, at 425 degrees for 30 to 35 minutes, until tender and golden.

Nutrition Per Serving: 91 calories, 1g fat, 0g sat fat, 0mg cholesterol, 6mg sodium, 18g carbohydrate, 2g fiber, 1g sugars, 2g protein.

Laurel Perry, *Loganville, GA*

Hearty Red Beans & Rice

My family loves beans and rice and this is the best recipe I have ever found!

Serves 8

16-oz. pkg. dried kidney beans
2 T. oil
1 onion, chopped
3 stalks celery, chopped
1 green pepper, chopped
2 cloves garlic, minced
3 c. water
2 ²/₃ c. low-sodium beef broth
¹/₂ t. red pepper flakes
1 meaty ham bone or ham hock
4 c. cooked brown rice
Garnish: chopped green onions, crisply
    cooked bacon

Soak beans overnight in water to cover; drain and set aside. In a large skillet, heat oil over medium-high heat. Add onion, celery, pepper and garlic; sauté until onion is translucent, 5 to 6 minutes. Place in a slow cooker along with drained beans, water, broth and red pepper flakes. Add ham bone and push down into mixture. Cover and cook on low setting until beans are very tender, 9 to 10 hours. Remove ham bone; dice meat and return to slow cooker. Serve beans spooned over hot cooked rice in bowls. Garnish with green onions and bacon.

Nutrition Per Serving: 452 calories, 11g fat, 2g sat fat, 35mg cholesterol, 521mg sodium, 60g carbohydrate, 11g fiber, 3g sugars, 30g protein.

Karen Hazelett, *Fremont, IN*

Kay's Sticky Chicken

This recipe is delicious and incredibly easy... make it the night before, pop it in the slow cooker and forget about it all day! It's one of my husband's favorite meals. I received this recipe from my good friend, Kay, and have shared it many times with co-workers.

Makes 8 servings

4-lb. roasting chicken
1 t. salt
2 t. paprika
1 t. cayenne pepper
1 t. onion powder
1 t. dried thyme
1 t. white pepper
¹/₂ t. garlic powder
¹/₂ t. pepper
1 onion, halved

Pat chicken dry with paper towels. Combine salt and spices in a small bowl. Rub mixture evenly onto chicken, both inside and out, making sure to rub deep into the skin. Insert onion halves into chicken. Place chicken in a large plastic zipping bag; seal and refrigerate overnight. In the morning, remove chicken from bag and place in a slow cooker. Do not add any water. Cover and cook on low setting for 8 to 10 hours.

Nutrition Per Serving: 254 calories, 11g fat, 3g sat fat, 107mg cholesterol, 429mg sodium, 1g carbohydrate, 0g fiber, 0g sugars, 36g protein.

Jennifer Brandes, *Leroy, NY*

Parmesan Zucchini & Spaghetti

We grew so much zucchini in our garden that I had to come up with some creative recipes!

Makes 6 servings

16-oz. pkg. spaghetti, uncooked
2 zucchini, cubed
2 yellow squash, cubed
½ c. onion, diced
1 clove garlic, minced
2 T. butter
½ c. 2 % milk
½ c. grated Parmesan cheese
pepper to taste

Cook spaghetti according to package directions; drain. Meanwhile, in a skillet over medium heat, sauté zucchini, squash, onion and garlic in butter until tender. Add milk and cheese to mixture in skillet; whisk until thickened into a sauce. Season with pepper. Serve zucchini mixture over spaghetti.

Nutrition Per Serving: 370 calories, 8g fat, 4g sat fat, 19mg cholesterol, 143mg sodium, 60g carbohydrate, 3g fiber, 4g sugars, 14g protein.

Jo Ann, *Gooseberry Patch*

Just Like Mom's Meatloaf

There is no better comfort food than meatloaf, and this is the best meatloaf ever!

Makes 7 servings

2 eggs, beaten
8-oz. can no-salt tomato sauce
¾ c. unsalted cracker crumbs
¼ c. onion, chopped
¼ c. green pepper, finely chopped
1 T. reduced-sodium Worcestershire sauce
½ t. salt
½ t. pepper
1⅓ lbs. extra-lean ground beef
½ c. low-sodium catsup
2 t. mustard
2 T. brown sugar, packed

Combine first 8 ingredients in a bowl; add ground beef and mix well. Shape into a loaf; place in an ungreased 9"x5" loaf pan. Bake, uncovered, at 350 degrees for one hour. Combine catsup, mustard and brown sugar; spoon over meatloaf and bake an additional 10 to 15 minutes.

Nutrition Per Serving: 241 calories, 9g fat, 3g sat fat, 101mg cholesterol, 331mg sodium, 18g carbohydrate, 1g fiber, 10g sugars, 21g protein.

Darrell Lawry, *Kissimmee, FL*

Roast Chicken with Vegetables

We love the flavor of thyme with roast chicken. You will too!

Serves 8

3¹/₂-lb. whole chicken
1 T. plus 1 t. olive oil, divided
1 t. dried thyme
¹/₄ t. salt
¹/₂ t. pepper
4 medium white onions, quartered
10 multi-colored or regular baby carrots
6 stalks celery, cut into 2-inch pieces
2 redskin potatoes, peeled and quartered

Roast Chicken with Vegetables

Place chicken in a large shallow roasting pan. Tie the legs together with kitchen string; insert meat thermometer into thickest part of thigh without touching bone. Rub chicken with one teaspoon oil; sprinkle with thyme, salt and pepper. Bake, uncovered, at 475 degrees for 15 minutes. Toss vegetables with remaining oil; arrange around chicken. Reduce oven to 400 degrees; bake chicken for an additional 35 to 45 minutes, until the internal temperature reaches 170 degrees.

Nutrition Per Serving: 195 calories, 7g fat, 1g sat fat, 45mg cholesterol, 171mg sodium, 16g carbohydrate, 3g fiber, 4g sugars, 17g protein.

Evelyn Moriarty, *Philadelphia, PA*

Vegetable Quinoa Patties

This recipe is my own, adapted from one I found online and tweaked. It has become a family favorite, especially in summertime when fresh-picked veggies are available.

Makes 6 servings

3 eggs
¹/₂ c. shredded part-skim mozzarella cheese
¹/₂ c. low-fat cottage cheese
¹/₄ c. whole-wheat flour
1 carrot, peeled and grated
1 zucchini, grated
3 T. green, red or yellow pepper, grated
3 green onions, finely chopped
¹/₂ t. ground cumin
¹/₄ t. garlic powder
¹/₈ t. salt

¹/₄ t. pepper
2 c. cooked quinoa
1 T. olive oil
Dilled Yogurt Dressing

Beat eggs in a large bowl; stir in cheeses and flour, blending well. Mix in vegetables. Combine seasonings; sprinkle over vegetable mixture and mix well. Add cooked quinoa; stir together well. Heat olive oil in a skillet over medium heat. With a small ladle, drop mixture into skillet, making 6 patties. Flatten lightly with ladle to about ¹/₄-inch thick. Fry patties for 4 to 5 minutes per side, until golden. Serve each patty with 3 tablespoons Dilled Yogurt Dressing.

DILLED YOGURT DRESSING:

¹/₂ c. plain Greek yogurt
1 cucumber, peeled and diced
3 sprigs fresh dill, snipped, or ¹/₂ t. dill weed

Stir together all ingredients in a small bowl.

Nutrition Per Serving: 230 calories, 10g fat, 3g sat fat, 104mg cholesterol, 302mg sodium, 23g carbohydrate, 4g fiber, 5g sugars, 13g protein.

Mom's Beef Stroganoff

Wendy Lee Paffenroth, *Pine Island, NY*

Mom's Beef Stroganoff

So rich and creamy, this recipe is a winner!

Serves 4

½ c. all-purpose flour
1 t. paprika
1 t. dry mustard
1 t. salt
½ t. pepper
1 ½ lbs. stew beef, sliced into strips
2 T. olive oil
1 onion, thinly sliced
¾ lb. sliced mushrooms
1 c. water
14 ½-oz. can low-sodium beef broth
½ c. plain low-fat yogurt
8-oz. pkg. wide egg noodles, cooked
Garnish: paprika, dried parsley

Combine flour and seasonings in a large plastic zipping bag. Add beef; seal and shake until all the meat is coated. Remove meat; reserve flour in plastic zipping bag. Heat oil in a Dutch oven over medium heat; brown meat on all sides. Add onion and mushrooms; sauté. Sprinkle with reserved flour; stir to mix. Add water and broth; stir. Reduce heat; cook for about one hour, until sauce is thickened and meat is tender. Remove from heat; stir in yogurt. Do not boil. Place noodles in large serving dish; spoon meat mixture over noodles. Sprinkle with paprika and parsley.

Nutrition Per Serving: 600 calories, 16g fat, 4g sat fat,151mg cholesterol, 898mg sodium, 48g carbohydrate, 2g fiber, 5g sugars, 64g protein.

Linda Karner, *Pisgah Forest, NC*

Shrimp Scampi & Asparagus

We love fresh asparagus when it comes in season, and I love finding new ways to use it.

Makes 6 servings

16-oz. pkg. linguine pasta, uncooked
1 T. salt
2 T. butter
2 T. olive oil
1 lb. asparagus, trimmed and cut into bite-size
    pieces
2 cloves garlic, minced
2 lbs. medium shrimp, peeled and cleaned
2 T. mixed fresh herbs like basil, thyme,
    oregano and chives, chopped
2 T. capers, drained
juice of ½ lemon
salt and pepper to taste
Garnish: shredded Parmesan cheese

Cook pasta according to package directions, adding salt to cooking water; drain when pasta is just tender. Meanwhile, in a large skillet over medium heat, melt butter with olive oil. Add asparagus and sauté until partially tender, about 5 minutes. Stir in garlic and shrimp. Cook until shrimp is bright pink, about 5 to 7 minutes. Add herbs, capers and lemon juice; heat through. Season with salt and pepper. Add pasta to mixture in skillet; toss well. If desired, sprinkle with Parmesan cheese.

Nutrition Per Serving: 521 calories, 12g fat, 4g sat fat, 257mg cholesterol, 625mg sodium, 61g carbohydrate, 4g fiber, 4g sugars, 44g protein.

Cilantro Chicken Skillet

Gail Blain Prather, *Stockton, KS*

Cilantro Chicken Skillet

This recipe is a winner for two reasons...I can use my favorite cast-iron skillet, and it's so fun to make and serve it in tortilla bowls!

Makes 4 servings

Tortilla Bowls
1 c. long-cooking rice, uncooked
3 T. canola oil, divided
1 lb. boneless, skinless chicken breasts, cubed
1 T. fresh cilantro, chopped
1 T. garlic, finely minced
1 c. onion, chopped
1/2 red pepper, chopped
15-oz. can red beans, drained and rinsed
3 c. shredded lettuce
Optional: additional chopped cilantro
hot pepper sauce

Make Tortilla Bowls; set aside. Cook rice according to package directions; keep warm. Meanwhile, in a large skillet over medium-high heat, heat oil. Add chicken, cilantro and garlic. Cook, stirring occasionally, until chicken is no longer pink, about 10 minutes. Remove chicken from skillet; keep warm. Heat remaining oil in same skillet; add onion and pepper. Cook, stirring occasionally, until onion is softened, about 4 minutes. Stir in beans and rice. Continue cooking, stirring occasionally, until heated through. To serve, place lettuce in bottom of prepared Tortilla Bowl. Spoon rice mixture on top and add chicken. Serve with hot sauce.

TORTILLA BOWLS:

For each bowl, use one 10-inch flour tortilla. Spray each side of the tortilla with cooking oil spray. Set desired number of oven-proof soup bowls upside-down on a baking sheet. Drape tortilla over the outside of each bowl. Bake at 350 degrees for just a few minutes, until lightly golden. Let stand until cooled before removing from soup bowls.

Nutrition Per Serving: 751 calories, 18g fat, 3g sat fat, 65mg cholesterol, 768mg sodium, 101g carbohydrate, 11g fiber, 6g sugars, 44g protein.

Stephanie Westfall, *Dallas, GA*

Pepper Steak

A family favorite! Sprinkle with chow mein noodles if you like a crunchy topping.

Makes 6 servings

1 1/2 to 2 lbs. beef round steak, sliced into strips
15-oz. can diced tomatoes
2 red peppers, sliced
1 onion, chopped
4-oz. can sliced mushrooms, drained
1/4 c. salsa
cooked rice

Mix all ingredients except rice in a slow cooker. Cover and cook on low setting for 6 to 8 hours. To serve, spoon over cooked rice.

Nutrition Per Serving: 186 calories, 4g fat, 1g sat fat, 68mg cholesterol, 336mg sodium, 9g carbohydrate, 3g fiber, 5g sugars, 28g protein.

Nancie Flynn, *Bear Creek Township, PA*

Gram's Zucchini in a Pan

Gram used to serve this as a main dish in late summer when zucchini was plentiful.

Makes 6 servings

2 T. olive oil
1 onion, thinly sliced and separated into rings
4 to 5 sweet Italian peppers, sliced
2 zucchini, thinly sliced
2 tomatoes, diced
1 t. Italian seasoning
salt and pepper to taste
³/₄ c. low-fat shredded Cheddar cheese

Heat olive oil in a skillet over medium heat. Add onion and peppers; cover and cook until soft, about 5 minutes. Stir in zucchini, tomatoes and seasonings. Cover and cook to desired tenderness. Remove from heat; stir in cheese. Cover and let stand until cheese melts; serve warm.

Nutrition Per Serving: 95 calories, 7g fat, 2g sat fat, 8mg cholesterol, 105mg sodium, 4g carbohydrate, 1g fiber, 2g sugars, 5g protein.

Jill Ball, *Highland, UT*

Cranberry Pork Chops

One of our favorite meals! So easy to prepare, but it looks and tastes likes you put a lot of time into it. I first tried it during the holiday season, and my family loved it so much that I now serve it several times a year.

Makes 6 servings

6 pork chops
¹/₄ t. salt
pepper to taste
16-oz. can jellied cranberry sauce
¹/₂ c. cranberry juice cocktail or apple juice
¹/₄ c. sugar
2 T. spicy mustard
¹/₄ c. cold water
2 T. cornstarch

Season pork chops with salt and pepper; place in a slow cooker. Combine cranberry sauce, juice, sugar and mustard in a bowl; pour over pork chops. Cover and cook on high setting for 6 to 8 hours. Shortly before serving time, remove pork chops to a platter; keep warm. Combine cold water and cornstarch in a saucepan. Cook over medium heat, stirring continuously, until mixture becomes thick. Add liquid from slow cooker to saucepan and boil until thickened. Serve pork chops with sauce.

Nutrition Per Serving: 343 calories, 4g fat, 1g sat fat, 74mg cholesterol, 547mg sodium, 43g carbohydrate, 1g fiber, 39g sugars, 35g protein.

Ann Hole, *South Australia, Australia*

Ann's Veggie Boats

We all love this dish when we barbecue... my family & friends always ask for seconds!

Makes 6 servings

6 zucchini
1 onion, finely chopped
1 clove garlic, pressed
2 t. butter
1 T. all-purpose flour
1/2 c. milk
1 c. shredded low-fat Cheddar cheese
15-oz. bag frozen mixed vegetables
1 T. fresh dill, chopped
1 T. capers, drained
2 slices bacon, finely chopped and crisply
   cooked
2 T. grated Parmesan cheese

Bring a stockpot of water to a boil over medium-high heat. Add zucchini and boil for 3 minutes; drain. Slice zucchini lengthwise; scoop out middles to form boats. In a saucepan over medium heat, sauté onion and garlic in butter until tender. Stir in flour; continue cooking for one minute, stirring constantly. Gradually stir in milk. Continue to stir until sauce boils and thickens. Add Cheddar cheese, vegetables, dill and capers. Fill zucchini boats with vegetable mixture. Top with bacon and Parmesan cheese. Arrange on an ungreased baking sheet and tent loosely with aluminum foil. Bake at 350 degrees until filling is heated through, about 20 to 25 minutes.

Nutrition Per Serving: 212 calories, 10g fat, 5g sat fat, 21mg cholesterol, 290mg sodium, 20g carbohydrate, 5g fiber, 7g sugars, 13g protein.

Jennie Gist, *Gooseberry Patch*

Chicken & Snow Pea Stir-Fry

Delicious! Also try this recipe with beef sirloin instead of chicken, diced fresh tomatoes and even Japanese-style buckwheat noodles. Quick and satisfying.

Makes 4 servings

8-oz. pkg. medium egg noodles, uncooked
3/4 c. orange juice
3 T. low-sodium soy sauce
4 t. cornstarch
1 T. brown sugar, packed
1/2 t. ground ginger
1 lb. boneless, skinless chicken breast, thinly
   sliced
2 t. canola oil
14 1/2-oz. can diced tomatoes
2 c. snow peas, trimmed

Cook noodles according to package directions; drain. Meanwhile, in a small bowl, combine orange juice, soy sauce, cornstarch, brown sugar and ginger; mix well and set aside. In a wok or large skillet over medium-high heat, cook and stir chicken in oil for 2 minutes, or until golden. Drain; add orange juice mixture and tomatoes with juice to skillet. Cook and stir until mixture is thickened. Add snow peas; cook and stir for 2 minutes, or until crisp-tender. Serve chicken mixture over hot noodles.

Nutrition Per Serving: 272 calories, 5g fat, 1g sat fat, 73mg cholesterol, 593mg sodium, 27g carbohydrate, 2g fiber, 12g sugars, 30g protein.

Arugula Potato Cornugula

Kelley Nicholson, *Gooseberry Patch*

Arugula Potato Cornugula

A fast and easy recipe. Let your kids help you toss in the ingredients one by one, and with each ingredient come up with a silly word that rhymes with arugula. They're sure to give this side dish a try!

Makes 4 servings

2 T. butter
1 t. garlic, minced
6 new redskin potatoes, sliced
1/4 t. salt
1/4 t. pepper
1 c. frozen corn
1/2 c. frozen lima beans
1 c. fresh arugula, torn
salt and pepper to taste

Melt butter in a large skillet over medium heat; cook garlic until tender. Stir in potatoes and seasoning. Cover and cook until tender, about 10 minutes, turning occasionally. Add corn and beans; cook until potatoes are tender, about 8 to 10 minutes. Season with salt and pepper. Add arugula; cover and let stand until arugula is wilted.

Nutrition Per Serving: 341 calories, 7g fat, 4g sat fat, 15mg cholesterol, 197mg sodium, 63g carbohydrate, 6g fiber, 6g sugars, 9g protein.

Karen Lee Puchnick, *Butler, PA*

Artichoke Frittata

This simple recipe makes a quick weeknight meal. The eggs provide the protein. Serve it with a big tossed salad and slices of whole-grain toast. Yummy!

Makes 8 servings

2 6-oz. jars marinated artichokes, drained and 2 T. marinade reserved
4 eggs, beaten
1 c. ricotta cheese
1 onion, chopped
1/8 t. dried rosemary
1/8 t. dried thyme
1/8 t. dried basil
1/8 t. dried marjoram

Finely chop artichokes; place in a bowl. Add reserved marinade and remaining ingredients; mix well. Spread mixture evenly into a greased 8"x8" baking pan. Bake at 350 degrees for about 30 minutes, or until set and golden. Cut into rectangles; serve warm.

Nutrition Per Serving: 124 calories, 8g fat, 4g sat fat, 108mg cholesterol, 84mg sodium, 4g carbohydrate, 2g fiber, 0g sugars, 8g protein.

Happy Presentation
······· * ·······

Serve these frittatas on a large square plate surrounded with fresh herbs. Prepare a side salad for each person on matching smaller plates for a very pretty presentation.

Mom's Fall-Apart Sunday Roast

Karla Neese, *Edmond, OK*

Mom's Fall-Apart Sunday Roast

Everyone will love this tender roast surrounded with colorful veggies!

Serves 6

3-lb. boneless beef chuck roast
salt, pepper and garlic powder to taste
1 T. canola oil
4 potatoes, peeled and quartered
1 onion, quartered
4 carrots, peeled and cut into chunks
1 lb. fresh green beans, trimmed and halved
1 c. water

Sprinkle roast with salt, pepper and garlic powder to taste. Heat oil in a skillet; brown roast on all sides. Place potatoes in a slow cooker; place roast on top of potatoes. Add onions, carrots and green beans. Add water and cover. Cook on low setting for 6 to 8 hours.

Nutrition Per Serving: 584 calories, 29g fat, 12g sat fat, 156mg cholesterol, 225mg sodium, 33g carbohydrate, 6g fiber, 7g sugars, 48g protein.

Jo Ann, *Gooseberry Patch*

Easy Poached Salmon

An elegant dinner for guests...or treat your family! I like to serve tender roasted asparagus with this salmon.

Makes 4 servings

1 c. water
½ c. vegetable broth
½ c. onion, sliced
2 sprigs fresh parsley, snipped
5 peppercorns
¼ t. salt
1 lb. salmon fillets
Creamy Dijon Sauce

In a one-quart microwave-safe dish, combine all ingredients except fish; stir well. Cover with plastic wrap. Microwave on high for 2 to 3 minutes, until mixture boils. Discard peppercorns, if desired. Place fish in a separate microwave-safe dish. Pour mixture over fish. Cover and microwave on medium-high for 5 to 6 minutes, until fish flakes easily with a fork. Carefully remove fish to a serving plate. Serve immediately, or chill and serve cold. Serve with Creamy Dijon Sauce.

CREAMY DIJON SAUCE:
½ c. plain Greek yogurt
1 T. Dijon mustard
1 T. lemon juice
2 t. fresh dill, chopped

Combine all ingredients; mix well and chill before serving.

Nutrition Per Serving: 266 calories, 16g fat, 4g sat fat, 64mg cholesterol, 390mg sodium, 4g carbohydrate, 1g fiber, 2g sugars, 26g protein.

Melinda's Veggie Stir-Fry

Melinda Daniels, *Lewiston, ID*

Melinda's Veggie Stir-Fry

I really like stir-fry and chow mein, so I created this recipe using the items that I had in my garden and fridge. It is now one of my family's favorites and makes great leftovers.

Serves 8

8-oz. pkg. spaghetti, uncooked
2 c. broccoli, cut into bite-size flowerets
1 c. snow or sugar snap pea pods, halved
2 carrots, peeled and thinly sliced
½ onion, thinly sliced
¼ green pepper, thinly sliced
Stir-Fry Sauce

Cook spaghetti as package directs; drain and set aside. Meanwhile, place vegetables into a steamer basket; place in a large stockpot filled with enough water to just reach the bottom of the basket. Heat over medium heat and steam for about 3 to 5 minutes, until just beginning to soften; drain. If crisper vegetables are desired, omit this step. When spaghetti and vegetables are done, add to Stir-Fry Sauce in skillet. Cook and stir over medium-high heat for about 15 minutes, to desired tenderness.

STIR-FRY SAUCE:

½ c. olive oil
⅓ c. low-sodium soy sauce
2 T. Dijon mustard
2 T. sliced pepperoncini, chopped
2 cloves garlic, minced
1 t. pepper

In a large skillet over low heat, mix all ingredients together. Simmer until sauce is heated through.

Nutrition Per Serving: 257 calories, 14g fat, 2g sat fat, 0mg cholesterol, 415mg sodium, 27g carbohydrate, 3g fiber, 3g sugars, 6g protein.

Mary Gage, *Wakewood, CA*

Italian Orange Roughy

Once marinated, this microwave dinner is ready in under 10 minutes!

Serves 4

1 lb. orange roughy fillets
½ c. tomato juice
2 T. white vinegar
.7-oz. pkg. Italian salad dressing mix
¼ c. green onions, chopped
¼ c. green pepper, chopped

Place fish fillets in a shallow 2-quart microwave-safe dish. Combine tomato juice, vinegar and salad dressing mix. Pour over fish. Cover and refrigerate for 30 minutes. Uncover; sprinkle with onions and pepper. Microwave, covered, on high for 3 minutes. Turn fish, cover again and cook 2 to 4 minutes longer, until fish flakes easily. Let cooked fish stand for 2 minutes before uncovering.

Nutrition Per Serving: 97 calories, 1g fat, 0g sat fat, 68mg cholesterol, 165mg sodium, 2g carbohydrate, 1g fiber, 1g sugars, 19g protein.

Tuscan Pork Loin

Gina McClenning, *Valrico, FL*

Tuscan Pork Loin

Guests always ask for this recipe. It makes a lot, but leftovers are delicious the next day. Instead of using plain cream cheese, try garlic-and-herb spreadable cheese.

Serves 10

4-lb. boneless pork tenderloin roast
8-oz. pkg. light cream cheese, softened
1 T. dried pesto seasoning
½ c. baby spinach
4 slices bacon, crisply cooked
12-oz. jar roasted red peppers, drained and divided
1 t. paprika
½ t. salt
½ t. pepper
Garnish: baby spinach

Slice pork lengthwise, cutting down center, but not through other side. Open halves and cut down center of each half, cutting to, but not through other sides. Open pork into a rectangle. Place pork between 2 sheets of heavy-duty plastic wrap and flatten into an even thickness using a rolling pin or the flat side of a meat mallet. Spread cream cheese evenly over pork. Sprinkle with pesto seasoning; arrange spinach over cream cheese. Top with bacon slices and half of red peppers; reserve remaining red peppers for another recipe. Roll up pork lengthwise; tie at 2-inch intervals with kitchen string. Rub pork with paprika, salt and pepper. Place roast seam-side down on a lightly greased rack on an aluminum foil-lined baking sheet.

Bake at 425 degrees for 30 minutes, or until a meat thermometer inserted into thickest portion registers 145 degrees. Remove from oven; let stand for 10 minutes. Remove string from pork; slice pork into ½-inch thick servings. Serve pork slices on a bed of spinach leaves, if desired.

Nutrition Per Serving: 292 calories, 12g fat, 5g sat fat, 120mg cholesterol, 1008mg sodium, 4g carbohydrate, 0g fiber, 1g sugars, 43g protein.

Jen Licon-Connor, *Gooseberry Patch*

Market-Fresh Carrots

A zippy side dish...ready in only 10 minutes! Yes, it is easy, but it is oh-so-good!

Serves 4

1 T. olive oil
3 c. baby carrots
1½ T. balsamic vinegar
1 T. brown sugar, packed

Heat oil in a skillet over medium heat. Add carrots; sauté for 10 minutes, or until tender. Stir in vinegar and brown sugar; toss to coat.

Nutrition Per Serving: 88 calories, 4g fat, 1g sat fat, 0mg cholesterol, 69mg sodium, 14g carbohydrate, 3g fiber, 9g sugars, 1g protein.

Chapter Six

Room for Dessert

Sit back and enjoy **Sweet Guilt-Free Goodies** that come right from your kitchen. Fresh and pretty Strawberry Pie comes together quickly and will be the star of the show! Grandmother's Goofy Cupcakes are so rich and chocolatey that they don't need any frosting. Want a classic dessert? Present Easy Cherry Cobbler to your family and watch the smiles. Everyone loves cookies! Whip up a batch of Chocolate Chip-Oat Cookies for a quick grab on the way out the door. So find the sweet treat that feeds your need and enjoy every bite!

Melissa Luck, *West Plains, MO*

Peach Flip-Overs

I had so many peaches from the farmers' market that I popped the extras in the freezer. Try them with peach ice cream...perfect for this recipe!

Makes 8 servings

2 to 3 peaches, pitted, peeled and sliced
2 t. butter
¼ t. nutmeg
1 t. cinnamon
2 to 3 T. pumpkin pie spice
1 t. brown sugar, packed
¼ c. sugar
1 to 2 t. vanilla extract
8-oz. tube refrigerated crescent rolls
ground ginger to taste
Garnish: powdered sugar, cinnamon

Add peaches, butter, spices, sugars and vanilla to a saucepan over medium heat. Simmer for 10 minutes; reduce heat to low. Separate and arrange crescent roll dough on a lightly greased baking sheet; sprinkle with ginger. Bake at 375 degrees for 5 minutes. Remove from oven and top each with one tablespoon peach mixture. Roll into a crescent; secure with a toothpick. Return to the oven for 5 to 10 minutes, or until golden. Sprinkle with powdered sugar and cinnamon.

Nutrition Per Serving: 149 calories, 6g fat, 3g sat fat, 3mg cholesterol, 210mg sodium, 22g carbohydrate, 1g fiber, 13g sugars, 2g protein.

Deborah Goodrich, *Smithfield, VA*

Deborah's Blueberry Cake

All my friends call me "Betty Crocker" because I love to cook and share. Whenever I bake this blueberry cake, they all make sure to get a slice of it!

Makes 24 servings

1 c. butter, softened
2 c. sugar
4 eggs, room temperature
1 t. vanilla extract
3 c. all-purpose flour
1 t. baking powder
½ t. salt
2 c. blueberries
2 t. lemon zest
Garnish: lemon rind curls, raw or coarse sugar

In a large bowl, beat together butter and sugar. Add eggs, one at a time, beating well after each addition. Beat until fluffy and add vanilla. In a separate bowl, mix together flour, baking powder and salt. Set aside one cup of flour mixture. Add remaining flour mixture to butter mixture and beat well. Dredge berries and lemon zest in reserved flour mixture. Gently fold berry mixture into batter. Spoon into a greased and floured 10" tube pan. Sprinkle raw or coarse sugar on top. Bake at 350 degrees for 1¼ hours, or until a cake tester inserted near the center comes out clean.

Nutrition Per Serving: 208 calories, 9g fat, 5g sat fat, 51mg cholesterol, 78mg sodium, 30g carbohydrate, 1g fiber, 18g sugars, 3g protein.

Deborah's Blueberry Cake

Shannon Sitko, *Warren, OH*

Grandmother's Waffle Cookies

My Grandmother Blanche always made these delicious cookies...we loved them!

Makes 3 dozen, serves 36

1 c. butter, melted and slightly cooled
4 eggs, beaten
1 c. sugar
1 c. brown sugar, packed
2 t. vanilla extract
4 c. all-purpose flour
Optional: frosting and sprinkles

Mix together melted butter, eggs and sugars; add vanilla. Slowly stir in flour. Drop batter by teaspoonfuls onto a preheated ungreased waffle iron. Check cookies after about one minute. Cookies are done when they are a medium golden in center and light golden at the edges. Dip in frosting and sprinkles if desired.

Nutrition Per Serving: 148 calories, 6g fat, 3g sat fat, 34mg cholesterol, 11mg sodium, 22g carbohydrate, 0g fiber, 12g sugars, 2g protein.

Beth Bundy, *Long Prairie, MN*

Brandon's Pumpkin Squares

My son Brandon loves anything with pumpkin in it...he requests this dessert all year 'round! His love for these bars makes them very special to me.

Serves 20

12-oz. can evaporated milk
3 eggs, beaten
2 t. pumpkin pie spice
$\frac{1}{2}$ t. salt
1 c. sugar
15-oz. can pumpkin
18$\frac{1}{2}$-oz. pkg. yellow cake mix
$\frac{1}{2}$ c. butter, sliced
Garnish: whipped topping

Combine all ingredients except cake mix, butter and garnish. Pour into a greased 13"x11" pan. Sprinkle on dry cake mix; do not stir. Dot with butter. Bake at 350 degrees for 30 to 35 minutes. Serve with whipped topping.

Nutrition Per Serving: 193 calories, 5g fat, 3g sat fat, 37mg cholesterol, 282mg sodium, 35g carbohydrate, 1g fiber, 24g sugars, 3g protein.

Kitchen Helper

To keep your spices in order, group them by size of container and then put them in alphabetical order...no more frustration searching for the right spice.

Jennie Wiseman, *Coshocton, OH*

Hot Cinnamon Pudding

I used to make this cozy pudding for my girls when they were little. They would sled down a tiny hill in front of our home with their dad. When they came back in, they warmed up with this pudding.

Serves 8

1 ¼ c. brown sugar, packed
1 ½ c. cold water
¼ c. butter, melted and divided
¾ c. sugar
1 c. 2 % milk
2 c. all-purpose flour
2 t. baking powder
2 t. cinnamon
¼ t. salt
Optional: chopped nuts
Garnish: low-fat vanilla ice cream

Mix together brown sugar, cold water and 2 tablespoons butter. Pour into a greased and floured 1½ quart casserole dish. In a bowl, mix together remaining ingredients except nuts and garnish. Pour over brown sugar mixture. Top with nuts, if desired. Bake at 350 degrees for 45 minutes. Garnish as desired; serve warm.

Nutrition Per Serving: 384 calories, 7g fat, 4g sat fat, 18mg cholesterol, 322mg sodium, 78g carbohydrate, 1g fiber, 54g sugars, 4g protein.

Gerry Donnella, *Boston, VA*

Tried & True Apple Casserole

My family loves these easy baked apples.

Serves 8

8 to 10 tart apples, peeled, cored and halved
½ c. sugar
1 T. all-purpose flour
½ t. cinnamon
¼ t. nutmeg
1 T. butter, diced
Optional: golden raisins, chopped walnuts

Place apples in a greased 2-quart casserole dish; set aside. Mix together dry ingredients; sprinkle over apples. Dot with butter. Sprinkle with raisins and walnuts, if desired. Cover and bake at 350 degrees for 45 minutes to one hour.

Nutrition Per Serving: 190 calories, 2g fat, 1g sat fat, 4mg cholesterol, 2mg sodium, 43g carbohydrate, 5g fiber, 35g sugars, 1g protein.

Brenda's Fruit Crisp

Brenda Smith, *Delaware, OH*

Brenda's Fruit Crisp

Here's my favorite dessert recipe...it's a yummy way to use a bumper crop of peaches, apples or berries!

Serves 6

5 c. frozen peaches, apples or berries, thawed
    and juices reserved
1 T. sugar
½ c. long-cooking oats, uncooked
⅓ c. brown sugar, packed
¼ c. all-purpose flour
¼ t. vanilla extract
¼ t. nutmeg
¼ t. cinnamon
¼ c. unsweetened flaked coconut
⅓ c. butter, diced
Garnish: low-fat vanilla ice cream

Place fruit and reserved juices in an ungreased 2-quart casserole dish; stir in sugar and set aside. Mix oats, brown sugar, flour, vanilla and spices in a bowl. Stir in coconut. Add butter to oat mixture; mix with a fork until mixture is the texture of coarse crumbs. Sprinkle over fruit. Bake at 375 degrees for 30 to 35 minutes, until topping is golden and fruit is tender. Serve warm, topped with a scoop of ice cream.

Nutrition Per Serving: 275 calories, 13g fat, 8g sat fat, 27mg cholesterol, 6mg sodium, 39g carbohydrate, 4g fiber, 25g sugars, 4g protein.

Wendy Lee Paffenroth, *Pine Island, NY*

Pumpkin Biscotti

Slices of biscotti are so nice to give to a co-worker along with a tea bag...a welcome morning treat. Try a gingerbread muffin or quick bread mix too...scrumptious!

Serves 18

4 eggs, beaten
1 c. butter, melted and slightly cooled
1 t. vanilla extract
2 15.4-oz. pkgs. pumpkin muffin or quick
    bread mix
8-oz. pkg. milk chocolate chips, divided
1 to 3 T. all-purpose flour

In a large bowl, combine eggs, butter and vanilla; stir until well blended. Blend in dry muffin or quick bread mix and ½ cup chocolate chips; stir again. Mixture will be sticky. Add enough flour to form a smooth dough; knead on a lightly floured surface for several minutes. Divide dough in half; shape each half into an oval loaf and flatten slightly. Place on a lightly greased baking sheet and bake at 350 degrees for 30 to 40 minutes, or until golden. Remove from oven and set aside to cool 15 to 20 minutes. Using a serrated knife, cut loaves into ¾-inch-thick slices; arrange on baking sheet. Return to oven and continue to bake 15 minutes longer. Remove from oven and set aside to cool. Melt remaining chocolate chips and drizzle over slices; cool.

Nutrition Per Serving: 360 calories, 18g fat, 10g sat fat, 71mg cholesterol, 301mg sodium, 49g carbohydrate, 1g fiber, 24g sugars, 3g protein.

Chocolate Chip-Oat Cookies

Tracey Ten Eyck, *Austin, TX*

Chocolate Chip-Oat Cookies

This recipe was handed down to me by my mother, who is now ninety-five. She made the best homemade cookies ever!

Makes 4 dozen, serves 24

1 c. butter
3/4 c. brown sugar, packed
3/4 c. sugar
2 eggs
1 t. hot water
1 1/2 c. all-purpose flour
1 t. baking soda
1 t. salt
12-oz. pkg. semi-sweet chocolate chips
2 c. long-cooking oats, uncooked
Optional: 1 c. nuts, finely chopped
1 t. vanilla extract

In a large bowl, beat butter until soft. Gradually add sugars, blending until light and fluffy. Add eggs, one at a time, beating well after each addition. Stir in hot water. In a separate bowl, mix together flour, baking soda and salt; gradually add flour mixture to butter mixture. Stir in chocolate chips, oats and nuts, if desired; mix thoroughly. Add vanilla and blend well. Drop by 1/2 teaspoonfuls onto greased baking sheets. Bake at 375 degrees for 8 to 10 minutes, until tops are golden.

Nutrition Per Serving: 271 calories, 13g fat, 8g sat fat, 38mg cholesterol, 162mg sodium, 37g carbohydrate, 2g fiber, 13g sugars, 4g protein.

Mary Ann Saint, *Indian Land, SC*

Grandma Saint's Fridge Cookies

My sister-in-law in Louisiana always made these cookies for us when we visited. She knew my husband would be so happy to eat the cookies his mother used to make. In fact, it made all of us happy...they're the most delicious refrigerator cookies I've ever tasted. You can't eat just one...they are addictive!

Makes 4 dozen, serves 24

1 c. butter, softened
1/2 c. sugar
1/2 c. brown sugar, packed
1 egg, beaten
1 t. vanilla extract
2 c. all-purpose flour
1/2 t. baking soda
1/4 t. salt
1 c. chopped pecans

In a large bowl, blend butter and sugars. Add egg and vanilla; mix well. In a separate bowl, mix together remaining ingredients except pecans. Add flour mixture to butter mixture and stir well; add pecans. Divide dough into 2 parts. Form each part into a roll; wrap rolls in wax paper. Refrigerate at least 2 hours to overnight. Cut dough into 1/2-inch thick slices; arrange 2 inches apart on lightly greased baking sheets. Bake at 350 degrees for 14 to 15 minutes.

Nutrition Per Serving: 87 calories, 6g fat, 3g sat fat, 14mg cholesterol, 28mg sodium, 9g carbohydrate, 0g fiber, 4g sugars, 1g protein.

Grandmother's Goofy Cupcakes

Cathie Ellison, *Ontario, Canada*

Grandmother's Goofy Cupcakes

This chocolate cake recipe came from my grandmother to my mum to me. I believe it came about during the First World War when certain ingredients were hard to get.

Serves 12

1½ c. all-purpose flour
1 c. sugar
½ c. baking cocoa
1 t. baking powder
1 t. baking soda
½ t. salt
1 t. instant coffee granules
1 c. hot water
5 T. butter, melted
1 T. white vinegar
1 t. vanilla extract
Garnish: chocolate chips

Preheat oven to 400 degrees. In a large bowl, sift together flour, sugar, cocoa, baking powder, baking soda and salt; set aside. Dissolve coffee granules in hot water; add to flour mixture. Add butter, vinegar and vanilla; stir until well blended. Pour into 12 muffin cups. Place pan into preheated oven, then reduce heat to 350 degrees. Bake for 15 to 20 minutes, or until toothpick tests clean. Immediately place several chocolate chips on each cupcake.

Nutrition Per Serving: 195 calories, 6g fat, 4g sat fat, 13mg cholesterol, 246mg sodium, 33g carbohydrate, 1g fiber, 19g sugars, 2g protein.

Heather Plasterer, *Colorado Springs, CO*

Ranger Cookies

The scrumptious taste of these crunchy cookies will always take me back home. Mom made them often while we were growing up and took them along to lots of get-togethers. Yum!

Makes 3 dozen, serves 36

1 c. butter
¾ c. sugar
¾ c. brown sugar, packed
2 eggs, beaten
1 t. vanilla extract
2 c. all-purpose flour
1 t. baking powder
1 t. baking soda
½ t. salt
2 c. long-cooking oats, uncooked
2 c. crispy rice cereal
1 c. unsweetened flaked coconut

In a large bowl, blend together butter and sugars; beat in eggs and vanilla. In a separate bowl, mix together flour, baking powder, baking soda and salt; stir in oats, cereal and coconut. Add flour mixture to butter mixture; mix well. Drop by rounded teaspoonfuls onto ungreased baking sheets. Bake at 350 degrees for 10 minutes.

Nutrition Per Serving: 153 calories, 7g fat, 4g sat fat, 24mg cholesterol, 75mg sodium, 21g carbohydrate, 1g fiber, 9g sugars, 3g protein.

Amy Snyder, *White Oak, WV*

Healthy Oatmeal Apple Crisp

This quick recipe almost tastes too good to believe that it's good for you!

Makes 16 servings

6 c. tart apples, peeled, cored and sliced
¼ c. frozen apple juice concentrate, thawed
1 t. cinnamon, divided
¼ c. butter, softened
¾ c. quick-cooking oats, uncooked
¼ c. whole-wheat flour
¼ c. brown sugar, packed

In a bowl, combine apples, apple juice concentrate and ½ teaspoon cinnamon. Stir until well mixed. Spread in an 8"x8" baking pan sprayed with non-stick vegetable spray. In the same bowl, mix remaining cinnamon and other ingredients until crumbly; sprinkle over apples. Bake, uncovered, at 375 degrees for 40 to 50 minutes, until apples are tender and topping is golden. Serve warm.

Nutrition Per Serving: 116 calories, 4g fat, 2g sat fat, 8mg cholesterol, 3mg sodium, 21g carbohydrate, 3g fiber, 12g sugars, 2g protein.

Sharon Demers, *Delores, CO*

Cherry-Pecan Bread Pudding

This old-fashioned bread pudding recipe is one of our favorites.

Serves 12

2-lb. loaf French bread, cubed
6 c. 2% milk
½ c. plus 2 T. sugar, divided
6 eggs, beaten
2 t. vanilla extract
½ t. cinnamon
½ c. dried tart cherries
½ c. chopped pecans
¼ c. butter, melted

Spread bread cubes on a baking sheet; let dry overnight. Combine milk and 5 tablespoons sugar in a saucepan over low heat. Heat to 120 degrees on a candy thermometer; remove from heat. Whisk together eggs, vanilla, cinnamon and remaining sugar in a large bowl. Stir in cherries and pecans. Slowly whisk half of milk mixture into egg mixture; add remaining milk mixture. Stir in bread cubes; toss to mix and let stand for 5 minutes. Mix in butter; transfer mixture to lightly greased 13"x9" baking pan. Bake at 350 degrees for 35 minutes, or until center is firm. Serve warm.

Nutrition Per Serving: 444 calories, 13g fat, 5g sat fat, 13mg cholesterol, 483mg sodium, 65g carbohydrate, 2g fiber, 23g sugars, 17g protein.

Cherry-Pecan Bread Pudding

Debra Boyd, *Gibsonia, PA*

Peanut Butter Brownies

These are my kids' favorite treats. I always used to make them for camping and picnics. Even though my kids now are in their twenties and are on their own, from time to time they still ask me to make them a pan of these yummy brownies!

Makes 2 dozen, serves 24

1/2 c. creamy peanut butter
1/4 c. butter, softened
1 t. vanilla extract
1 c. brown sugar, packed
2 eggs
2/3 c. all-purpose flour

Blend together peanut butter, butter, vanilla and brown sugar. Add eggs, one at a time, beating well after each addition. Stir in flour. Spread batter evenly in a well-greased 8"x8" baking pan. Bake at 350 degrees for 20 to 30 minutes, until center tests done with a toothpick. Do not overbake. Cool; cut into bars.

Nutrition Per Serving: 69 calories, 5g fat, 2g sat fat, 21mg cholesterol, 32mg sodium, 4g carbohydrate, 0g fiber, 1g sugars, 2g protein.

Happy Presentation

Cut bar cookies into small squares
and slide them into parchment bags
for a quick take-along treat.

Lauren Williams, *Kewanee, MO*

Coconut Cream Pie

This pie is a work of art...and so delicious!

Serves 10

2 c. 2 %milk
1/3 c. sugar
1/4 c. cornstarch
1/4 t. salt
3 egg yolks, beaten
1 1/2 c. unsweetened flaked coconut, divided
2 T. butter, softened
1/2 t. vanilla extract
9-inch pie crust, baked
Meringue

Combine milk, sugar, cornstarch and salt in a large saucepan; cook over medium heat until thickened, stirring constantly. Remove from heat. Place egg yolks in a small bowl. Stir a small amount of hot milk mixture into egg yolks. Pour yolk mixture back into saucepan; simmer gently for 2 minutes. Stir in coconut, butter and vanilla Pour into crust. Spread Meringue over hot pie filling; seal to edges. Sprinkle with coconut. Bake at 350 degrees for 12 minutes, or until golden.

MERINGUE:

4 egg whites
7-oz. jar marshmallow creme

Beat egg whites in a bowl with an electric mixer at high speed until stiff peaks form. Add marshmallow creme; beat for 2 minutes, or until well blended.

Nutrition Per Serving: 307 calories, 15g fat, 8g sat fat, 66mg cholesterol, 225mg sodium, 38g carbohydrate, 1g fiber, 19g sugars, 6g protein.

Coconut Cream Pie

Strawberry Pie

Darci Stavish, *Randall, MN*

Strawberry Pie

Take the whole family strawberry picking...
not only is it fun, but you'll have this fresh,
homemade pie to enjoy too!

Makes 8 to 10 servings

1 c. all-purpose flour
2 T. powdered sugar
1/2 c. butter, softened
1 1/2 c. water
3/4 c. sugar
1/8 t. salt
2 T. cornstarch
3-oz. pkg. strawberry gelatin mix
4 c. strawberries, hulled and halved
Optional: whipped topping

Combine flour and powdered sugar; cut butter
into flour mixture until dough resembles
coarse crumbs. Pat into a 9" pie plate; bake at
350 degrees for 15 minutes. Set aside to cool. In
a 2-quart saucepan, bring water, sugar, salt and
cornstarch to a boil until clear; stir in gelatin
until dissolved. Remove from heat; cool slightly.
Pour 1/4 of the gelatin mixture into pie crust. Fill
crust with strawberries; pour remaining gelatin
mixture over the top. Chill in refrigerator until
set; serve with whipped topping, if desired.

Nutrition Per Serving: 188 calories, 10g fat, 6g sat fat,
24mg cholesterol, 48mg sodium, 17g carbohydrate, 2g
fiber, 5g sugars, 9g protein.

Sharon Levandowski, *Hoosick Falls, NY*

Gram's Zucchini Cookies

When we have fresh zucchini in the garden,
we make extra batches of this favorite cookie
and freeze them for later. What a good way
to use our zucchini and have some goodies to
look forward to!

Makes 4 dozen cookies, serves 48

3/4 c. butter, softened
1 1/2 c. sugar
1 egg, beaten
1 t. vanilla extract
1 1/2 c. zucchini, grated
2 1/2 c. all-purpose flour
2 t. baking powder
1 t. cinnamon
1/2 t. salt
1 c. chopped walnuts or almonds
6-oz. pkg. semi-sweet chocolate chips

Blend together butter and sugar in a bowl; beat
in egg and vanilla. Stir in zucchini. In a separate
bowl, combine flour, baking powder, cinnamon
and salt; gradually add to butter mixture. Stir
in nuts and chocolate chips. Drop by heaping
teaspoonfuls onto greased baking sheets. Bake
at 350 degrees for 13 to 15 minutes, until golden.
Remove to wire racks to cool.

Nutrition Per Serving: 110 calories, 6g total fat, 3g sat fat,
12mg cholesterol, 47mg sodium, 14g carbohydrate, 1g fiber,
6g sugars, 1g protein.

Mary Jackson, *Fishers, IN*

Bragging-Rights Banana Pudding

This recipe was handed down from my wonderful mother-in-law. It is a definite crowd-pleaser!

Serves 15

5¼-oz. pkg. instant vanilla pudding mix
3 c. 2% milk
16-oz. container plain Greek yogurt
12-oz. container frozen light whipped topping, thawed
10-oz. pkg. vanilla wafers, divided
4 bananas, sliced and divided

In a bowl, with an electric mixer on low speed, beat dry pudding mix and milk for 2 to 3 minutes, until thickened. Beat in yogurt; fold in topping. Set aside several vanilla wafers. In a large deep bowl, layer half each of remaining wafers, bananas and pudding mixture. Repeat layering. Crush reserved wafers and sprinkle on top. Cover; chill until served.

Nutrition Per Serving: 248 calories, 8g fat, 0g sat fat, 4mg cholesterol, 251mg sodium, 39g carbohydrate, 1g fiber, 22g sugars, 7g protein.

> ### ⤳ Healthy Fact ⤳
>
> Bananas are naturally free of fat, cholesterol and sodium. Bananas provide a variety of vitamins and minerals including Vitamin B6 and potassium.

Janet Seabern, *Winona, MN*

Snowy Glazed Apple Squares

My mother used to make this dessert when I was a young girl. It is our family favorite!

Makes about 2 dozen, serves 24

2½ c. all-purpose flour
½ t. salt
1 c. shortening
2 eggs, separated
½ to ⅔ c. milk
1½ c. corn flake cereal, crushed
8 baking apples, peeled, cored and sliced
1 c. sugar
1 t. cinnamon
2 T. powdered sugar

In a bowl, mix flour and salt; cut in shortening. Beat egg yolks in a measuring cup; add enough milk to measure ⅔ cup. Add to flour mixture and mix lightly. Divide dough into 2 parts, one slightly larger than the other. Roll out larger portion into a 15-inch by 10-inch rectangle. Place on a lightly greased 15"x10" jelly-roll pan. Sprinkle evenly with cereal; arrange apple slices over cereal. Mix sugar and cinnamon; sprinkle over apples. Roll out remaining dough and place on top; seal edges and cut slits in top. Beat egg whites until foamy and spread over dough. Bake at 350 degrees for one hour. Cool slightly; Sift powdered sugar over top. Cut into squares.

Nutrition Per Serving: 198 calories, 9g fat, 4g sat fat, 20mg cholesterol, 69mg sodium, 27g carbohydrate, 1g fiber, 15g sugars, 2g protein.

Snowy Glazed Apple Squares

Charlotte's Sheet Cake

Terri Lock, *Waverly, MO*

Charlotte's Sheet Cake

My mother-in-law is famous for this cake in our family...all 22 grandchildren request it when we get together.

Makes 24 servings

$^3/_4$ c. butter
1 c. water
$^1/_4$ c. baking cocoa
2 c. all-purpose flour
1 c. sugar
1 t. baking soda
$^1/_8$ t. salt
$^1/_2$ c. low-fat buttermilk
2 eggs, beaten
Optional: chocolate frosting

Place butter, water and cocoa in a saucepan. Heat until butter melts; let cool. In a mixing bowl, combine flour, sugar, baking soda and salt; mix well. Add butter mixture, buttermilk and eggs to flour mixture; stir well. Spread in a greased 15"x10" jelly-roll pan. Bake at 400 degrees for 20 minutes. Drizzle with chocolate frosting if desired.

Nutrition Per Serving: 132 calories, 7g fat, 4g sat fat, 31mg cholesterol, 82mg sodium, 17g carbohydrate, 0g fiber, 9g sugars, 2g protein.

Debbie Blundi, *Kunkletown, PA*

"Free" Coconut Cookies

I call these my "free" cookies because they are sugar-free, fat-free and dairy-free.

Makes 16 cookies, serves 16

8 pitted dates
1 very ripe banana, sliced
$1^1/_2$ c. unsweetened flaked coconut
$^1/_8$ t. vanilla extract
$^1/_8$ t. pumpkin pie spice

Place dates in a small bowl; add enough water to cover. Let stand for 2 to 4 hours; drain. Place dates, banana, coconut, vanilla and spice in a food processor or blender. Process until smooth and mixture resembles cookie dough. If mixture is too dry, add a drop or 2 of water; if mixture is too sticky, add a little more coconut. Scoop dough by teaspoonfuls onto ungreased baking sheets, one inch apart. Bake at 325 degrees for 10 to 15 minutes, until tips of coconut start to brown on the bottom; cookies will not brown on top. Let cookies stand on baking sheet until cool; remove to a plate. Leave uncovered for the first day, so cookies don't get too moist.

Nutrition Per Serving: 66 calories, 3g fat, 0g sat fat, 2mg cholesterol, 2mg sodium, 12g carbohydrate, 2g fiber, 9g sugars, 1g protein.

Phyllis Laughrey, *Mount Vernon, OH*

Peanut Butter Strudel Pie

The best peanut butter pie! Topped with meringue, it's wonderful.

Makes 10 servings

1/3 c. powdered sugar
1/4 c. creamy peanut butter
9-inch refrigerated pie crust, baked
1/2 c. plus 4 T. sugar, divided
1/3 c. all-purpose flour
2 c. skim milk
3 eggs, separated
2 T. butter
1/2 t. vanilla extract
1/2 t. cream of tartar
Garnish: chopped peanuts

In a small bowl, combine powdered sugar and peanut butter to resemble coarse crumbs. Spread over bottom of pie crust. In a 2-quart saucepan, stir together 1/2 cup sugar and flour; gradually add milk. Bring mixture to a boil over medium heat, stirring constantly; cook and stir 5 minutes or until thickened. Remove from heat and set aside. In a small bowl, beat egg yolks and blend in a small amount of milk mixture; stir well. Return egg mixture to hot mixture in pan; cook and stir over low heat 3 minutes. Remove from heat and stir in butter and vanilla. Cover and set filling aside. In a medium bowl, beat egg whites and cream of tartar until foamy. Gradually beat in remaining sugar, one tablespoon at a time, beating until stiff peaks form. Reheat filling over medium heat, stirring constantly, just until hot. Pour hot filling over peanut butter crumbs in pie crust. Spread meringue over pie, being sure to touch edges of crust to seal. Sprinkle chopped peanuts over meringue if desired. Bake at 325 degrees for 25 minutes, until meringue is golden. Cool completely before serving.

Nutrition Per Serving: 200 calories, 8g fat, 2g sat fat, 47mg cholesterol, 120mg sodium, 29g carbohydrate, 1g fiber, 19g sugars, 4g protein.

Mary Warren, *Auburn, MI*

Favorite Chocolate Chippers

The instant pudding in this cookie makes it extra chewy and good!

Makes 3 dozen, serves 36

3/4 c. butter, softened
3/4 c. brown sugar, packed
1/2 c. sugar
2 eggs, beaten
1 t. vanilla extract
3.4-oz. pkg. instant vanilla pudding mix
2 c. all-purpose flour
1 c. quick-cooking oats, uncooked
1 t. baking soda
12-oz. pkg. semi-sweet chocolate chips
1/4 c. chopped pecans
Optional: pecan halves

In a large bowl, beat together butter and sugars. Beat in eggs and vanilla. Add dry pudding mix, flour, oats and baking soda; mix just until well blended. Fold in chocolate chips and nuts. Drop by tablespoonfuls onto greased baking sheets. Top each with a pecan half if desired. Bake at 350 degrees for 12 to 14 minutes.

Nutrition Per Serving: 157 calories, 7g fat, 4g sat fat, 20mg cholesterol, 80mg sodium, 22g carbohydrate, 1g fiber, 14g sugars, 2g protein.

Favorite Chocolate Chippers

Easy Cherry Cobbler

Melonie Klosterho, *Fairbanks, AK*

Easy Cherry Cobbler

If they're available, use fresh-from-the-farm pitted cherries for a special treat.

Serves 8

15-oz. can tart red cherries
1 c. all-purpose flour
1 c. sugar, divided
1 c. 2% milk
2 t. baking powder
$^1/_8$ t. salt
$^1/_4$ c. butter, melted
Optional: vanilla ice cream or whipped
   topping

Bring cherries with juice to a boil in a saucepan over medium heat; remove from heat. Mix flour, $^3/_4$ cup sugar, milk, baking powder and salt in a medium bowl. Pour butter into 6 one-cup ramekins or into a 2-quart casserole dish; pour flour mixture over butter. Add cherries; do not stir. Sprinkle remaining sugar over top. Bake at 400 degrees for 20 to 30 minutes. Serve warm with ice cream or whipped cream, if desired.

Nutrition Per Serving: 235 calories, 6g fat, 4g sat fat, 16mg cholesterol, 146mg sodium, 43g carbohydrate, 1g fiber, 31g sugars, 3g protein.

Bonnie Allard, *Santa Rosa, CA*

Peach Cobbler Muffins

My most requested muffins...I hope you like them as much as my family & friends do!

Makes 2 dozen, serves 24

3 c. all-purpose flour
1 c. sugar
$1^1/_2$ T. baking soda
$^1/_2$ t. salt
$^3/_4$ c. butter, diced
$1^3/_4$ c. 2 % milk
16-oz. can peaches, drained and chopped
Topping

Mix flour, sugar, baking soda and salt in a large bowl. Cut in butter with a pastry blender or fork until crumbly. Add milk and peaches; stir just until moistened. Fill greased or paper-lined muffin cups $^2/_3$ full. Spoon Topping onto muffins. Bake at 400 degrees for about 20 minutes, until golden and a toothpick inserted in the center comes out clean. Turn out and cool slightly on a wire rack; serve warm or cold.

TOPPING:

3 T. butter, diced
3 T. sugar
1 t. cinnamon

Mix all ingredients together with a pastry blender or fork in a small bowl until crumbly.

Nutrition Per Serving: 179 calories, 8g fat, 5g sat fat, 20mg cholesterol, 296mg sodium, 26g carbohydrate, 1g fiber, 13g sugars, 2g protein.

and corn syrup; beat just until blended. Sift together flour and spices. Dissolve baking soda in buttermilk; add the milk mixture to butter mixture alternately with flour mixture, stirring just until combined. Fill greased and floured muffin cups ²/₃ full. Bake at 350 degrees for 15 minutes, or until a toothpick inserted in center comes out clean.

Nutrition Per Serving: 137 calories, 5g fat, 3g sat fat, 31mg cholesterol, 69mg sodium, 20g carbohydrate, 0g fiber, 11g sugars, 2g protein.

Bernadette Dobias, *Houston, TX*

Emma's Gingerbread Muffins

If you like gingerbread cookies, you will love these yummy muffins!

Makes 2 ¹/₂ dozen, serves 30

³/₄ c. butter, softened
³/₄ c. sugar
3 eggs
¹/₂ c. molasses
2 T. light corn syrup
3 c. all-purpose four
2 t. cinnamon
2 t. ground ginger
1 t. nutmeg
1 t. baking soda
1 c. buttermilk

Place butter in a large bowl. Beat with an electric mixer at medium speed until creamy. Add sugar; beat just until combined. Add eggs, one at a time, beating after each addition. Add molasses

Cynthia Dodge, *Layton, UT*

Cynthia's Banana-Oatmeal Cookies

The combination of oatmeal and bananas makes these cookies so delicious!

Makes 4 dozen cookies, serves 48

³/₄ c. butter
1 c. sugar
1 egg, beaten
¹/₂ t. banana extract
¹/₄ c. wheat germ
5 bananas, sliced
2¹/₂ c. quick-cooking oats, uncooked
¹/₈ t. cinnamon
¹/₈ t. nutmeg
1¹/₂ c. all-purpose flour
¹/₂ t. baking soda
¹/₄ t. salt
Optional: 1 c. water, ¹/₂ to ³/₄ c. raisins

Beat butter and sugar together with an electric mixer on medium speed. Add egg and extract; blend well. Add wheat germ; blend. Stir in bananas, 2 cups oats, cinnamon and nutmeg;

blend well. Whisk together flour, baking soda and salt; stir into dough. If adding raisins, soak raisins in one cup of water for one minute; drain well and add to dough. Drop dough by teaspoonfuls onto parchment paper-lined baking sheets. Bake at 400 degrees for 11 to 13 minutes. Refrigerate any leftovers.

Nutrition Per Serving: 102 calories, 4g fat, 2g sat fat, 11mg cholesterol, 28mg sodium, 16g carbohydrate, 1g fiber, 6g sugars, 2g protein.

Sarah Oravecz, *Gooseberry Patch*

Walnut-Maple Streusel Cake

This cake keeps well, so you can bake it a day before and store it, wrapped in plastic.

Serves 12

2 c. all-purpose flour
1 t. baking powder
1 t. baking soda
$\frac{1}{2}$ t. salt
$\frac{1}{2}$ c. butter, room temperature
$\frac{3}{4}$ c. sugar
2 eggs, beaten
1 t. vanilla extract
8-oz. container plain Greek yogurt
Walnut Filling
Optional: powdered sugar

Whisk together flour, baking powder, baking soda and salt in a medium bowl; set aside. Beat butter and sugar in a large bowl with an electric mixer at medium-high speed until fluffy. Beat in eggs and vanilla. Beat in flour mixture alternately with yogurt, mixing just until blended. Spoon half of batter into a buttered and floured Bundt® pan. Spoon two-thirds of Walnut Filling over batter. Spread remaining batter over filling; smooth top. Dot with remaining filling. Bake at 350 degrees for 40 minutes, or until a toothpick inserted in center comes out clean. Cool cake in pan on a wire rack for 15 minutes. Run a knife around pan sides to loosen; turn cake out onto a serving platter and dust with powdered sugar, if desired.

WALNUT FILLING:

$\frac{1}{2}$ c. all-purpose flour
2 T. butter, softened
1 t. cinnamon
$1\frac{1}{4}$ c. chopped walnuts
$\frac{1}{2}$ c. maple syrup

Mix together flour, butter and cinnamon in a small bowl with a pastry blender or fork until crumbly. Stir in nuts and syrup.

Nutrition Per Serving: 367 calories, 19g fat, 7g sat fat, 57mg cholesterol, 226mg sodium, 44g carbohydrate, 2g fiber, 23g sugars, 8g protein.

Strawberry-Yogurt Mousse

Michelle Rooney, *Columbus, OH*

Strawberry-Yogurt Mousse

A very easy-to-make, refreshing dessert I've made for many years...you'll love it!

Makes 10 servings

2 8-oz. cartons strawberry yogurt
½ c. strawberries, hulled and crushed
8-oz. container frozen light whipped topping, thawed

Combine yogurt and strawberries; mix well. Fold in whipped topping; blend well. Spoon into cups or glasses. Place in refrigerator for 30 minutes before serving.

Nutrition Per Serving: 103 calories, 4g fat, 3g sat fat, 4mg cholesterol, 44mg sodium, 14g carbohydrate, 0g fiber, 6g sugars, 3g protein.

Kay Marone, *Des Moines, IA*

People-Pleasin' Peach Pie

There is nothing better than a homemade peach pie! Enjoy!

Serves 8

2 9-inch pie crusts
8 c. peaches, peeled, pitted and sliced
2 t. lemon juice
1 t. vanilla extract
½ c. sugar

6 T. cornstarch
1 t. cinnamon
¼ t. nutmeg
¼ t. salt
1 to 2 T. milk
Garnish: whipped topping

Line a 9" pie plate with one crust and set aside. Combine peaches, lemon juice and vanilla in a large bowl. Mix sugar, cornstarch, spices and salt in a separate bowl. Add sugar mixture to peach mixture; toss gently to coat. Spoon into pie crust. With a small cookie cutter, cut vents in remaining crust, reserving cut-outs. Place crust on top of pie; trim and seal edges. Brush milk over top crust and cut-outs; arrange cut-outs on crust. Cover edges loosely with aluminum foil. Bake at 400 degrees for 40 minutes. Remove foil and bake 10 to 15 more minutes, until crust is golden and filling is bubbly. Garnish with whipped topping.

Nutrition Per Serving: 364 calories, 15g fat, 4g sat fat, 0mg cholesterol, 310mg sodium, 54g carbohydrate, 4g fiber, 26g sugars, 4g protein.

5 to 6 minutes, until lightly golden. Cool. Frost using one tablespoon of frosting per cookie. Decorate as desired.

SIMPLE POWDERED SUGAR FROSTING:

3 c. powdered sugar
2 T. butter, melted
3 T. skim milk

Mix all ingredients together until smooth.

Nutrition Per Serving: 136 calories, 5g fat, 3g sat fat, 22mg cholesterol, 106mg sodium, 21g carbohydrate, 0g fiber, 14g sugars, 2g protein.

Dianna Hamilton, *Beaverton, OR*

Good Neighbor Sugar Cookies

These are the best sugar cookies ever!

Makes 3 dozen cookies, serves 36

3 c. all-purpose flour
1 t. cream of tartar
1 t. baking soda
1 t. salt
³/₄ c. butter
2 eggs, beaten
1 c. sugar
1 t. vanilla extract
Simple Powdered Sugar Frosting

Mix together flour, cream of tartar, baking soda and salt in a bowl. In a separate bowl, whisk together remaining ingredients with a fork. Stir butter mixture into flour mixture. Wrap dough in plastic wrap; refrigerate for 30 minutes. On a floured surface, roll out dough ¹/₈-inch thick; cut out with cookie cutters. Arrange on lightly greased baking sheets. Bake at 375 degrees for

---

Barb Lueck, *Prairie, MN*

Peach Melba Pie

Peaches and raspberries together...yum!

Serves 6

4 peaches, peeled, pitted and sliced
1 c. sugar
5 t. lemon juice
¹/₄ c. cornstarch
¹/₃ c. water
3 c. fresh raspberries
9-inch pie crust, baked

In a large saucepan over medium heat, combine peaches, sugar and lemon juice. In a small bowl, stir cornstarch and water until smooth; stir into peach mixture. Bring to a boil; cook and stir one minute, or until thickened. Remove from heat; cool to room temperature. Gently fold in raspberries; spoon into baked pie crust. Chill at least 3 hours to overnight.

Nutrition Per Serving: 380 calories, 11g fat, 3g sat fat, 0mg cholesterol, 165mg sodium, 70g carbohydrate, 6g fiber, 45g sugars, 4g protein.

Leisha Howard, *Seattle, WA*

Slow-Cooker Tapioca Pudding

This slow-cooker version of tapioca pudding that I remember as a child makes it so easy!

Serves 12

8 c. 2% milk
1 c. small pearl tapioca, uncooked
1 c. sugar
4 eggs, beaten
1 t. vanilla extract
½ t. almond extract
Garnish: whipped topping, sliced fresh fruit

Add milk, tapioca and sugar to a slow cooker; stir gently. Cover and cook on high setting for 3 hours. In a bowl, mix together eggs, extracts and 2 spoonfuls of hot milk mixture from slow cooker. Slowly stir mixture into slow cooker. Cover and cook on high setting for an additional 20 minutes. Chill overnight. Garnish as desired.

Nutrition Per Serving: 217 calories, 5g fat, 3g sat fat, 75mg cholesterol, 101mg sodium, 36g carbohydrate, 0g fiber, 25g sugars, 8g protein.

Kathleen Sturm, *Corona, CA*

Sweet Raspberry-Oat Bars

These layered bars with raspberry jam in the middle are my husband's favorite!

Makes 2 ½ dozen, serves 30

½ c. butter
1 c. brown sugar, packed
1½ c. all-purpose flour
½ t. baking soda
½ t. salt
1½ c. long-cooking oats, uncooked
¼ c. water
⅔ c. seedless raspberry jam
1 t. lemon juice

In a large bowl, blend together butter and brown sugar until fluffy; set aside. Combine flour, baking soda and salt in a separate bowl. Stir flour mixture into butter mixture. Add oats and water; mix together until crumbly. Firmly pat half of oat mixture into the bottom of a greased 13"x9" baking pan. In a small bowl, stir together jam and lemon juice; spread over oat mixture. Sprinkle remaining oat mixture over top. Bake at 350 degrees for 25 minutes. Cool completely before cutting into bars.

Nutrition Per Serving: 128 calories, 4g fat, 2g sat fat, 8mg cholesterol, 65mg sodium, 22g carbohydrate, 1g fiber, 11g sugars, 2g protein.

Sharon Jones, *Oklahoma City, OK*

Estelle's Baked Custard

So rich and creamy, this baked custard is a family favorite!

Serves 8

6 eggs
6 c. 2% milk
1/2 c. sugar
1 1/2 t. vanilla extract
1/8 t. salt
Garnish: whipped topping, cinnamon or
    nutmeg

Whisk eggs until well beaten in a large bowl. Add milk, sugar, vanilla and salt; whisk well. Pour into 8 ungreased custard cups. Set cups in a rimmed baking pan. Pour an inch of hot water into baking pan. Bake at 325 degrees for one hour, or until a knife inserted in center comes out clean. Garnish with whipped topping, cinnamon or nutmeg. Cool at room temperature or in refrigerator 1 1/2 to 2 hours before serving.

Nutrition Per Serving: 197 calories, 7g fat, 3g sat fat, 154mg cholesterol, 177mg sodium, 22g carbohydrate, 0g fiber, 22g sugars, 11g protein.

Jill Ball, *Highland, UT*

Sweet Apple Tarts

I like to use Granny Smith apples in these tarts, but you can use any good baking apple that you like.

Serves 9

1 sheet frozen puff pastry, thawed
1/2 c. apricot jam
4 Granny Smith apples, peeled, cored and very
    thinly sliced
1/4 c. brown sugar, packed
1/2 t. cinnamon
1/2 c. pistachio nuts, chopped
Optional: vanilla ice cream

Roll pastry into a 12-inch square on a lightly floured surface. Cut pastry into nine 3-inch squares. Arrange squares on an ungreased baking sheet; pierce with a fork. Spoon jam evenly over each square; arrange apple slices over jam. Combine brown sugar and cinnamon in a small bowl; mix well. Sprinkle over apple slices. Bake at 400 degrees for 20 to 25 minutes, until pastry is golden and apples are crisp-tender. Sprinkle with nuts. Serve warm topped with scoops of ice cream, if desired.

Nutrition Per Serving: 289 calories, 14g fat, 3g sat fat, 0mg cholesterol, 77mg sodium, 41g carbohydrate, 2g fiber, 22g sugars, 4g protein.

Sweet Apple Tarts

Index

Index

U.S. to Metric Recipe Equivalents

Volume Measurements

¼ teaspoon . . . . 1 mL
½ teaspoon . . . . 2 mL
1 teaspoon . . . . 5 mL
1 tablespoon = 3 teaspoons . . . . 15 mL
2 tablespoons = 1 fluid ounce . . . . 30 mL
¼ cup . . . . 60 mL
⅓ cup . . . . 75 mL
½ cup = 4 fluid ounces . . . . 125 mL
1 cup = 8 fluid ounces . . . . 250 mL
2 cups = 1 pint = 16 fluid ounces . . 500 mL
4 cups = 1 quart . . . . 1 L

Weights

1 ounce . . . . 30 g
4 ounces . . . . 120 g
8 ounces . . . . 225 g
16 ounces = 1 pound . . . . 450 g

Baking Pan Sizes

Square

8x8x2 inches . . . . 2 L = 20x20x5 cm
9x9x2 inches . . . . 2.5 L = 23x23x5 cm

Rectangular

13x9x2 inches . . . . 3.5 L = 33x23x5 cm

Loaf

9x5x3 inches . . . . 2 L = 23x13x7 cm

Round

8x1½ inches . . . . 1.2 L = 20x4 cm
9x1½ inches . . . . 1.5 L = 23x4 cm

Recipe Abbreviations

t. = teaspoon   ltr. = liter
T. = tablespoon   oz. = ounce
c. = cup   lb. = pound
pt. = pint   doz. = dozen
qt. = quart   pkg. = package
gal. = gallon   env. = envelope

Oven Temperatures

300° F . . . . 150° C
325° F . . . . 160° C
350° F . . . . 180° C
375° F . . . . 190° C
400° F . . . . 200° C
450° F . . . . 230° C

Kitchen Measurements

A pinch = ⅛ tablespoon
1 fluid ounce = 2 tablespoons
3 teaspoons = 1 tablespoon
4 fluid ounces = ½ cup
2 tablespoons = ⅛ cup
8 fluid ounces = 1 cup
4 tablespoons = ¼ cup
16 fluid ounces = 1 pint
8 tablespoons = ½ cup
32 fluid ounces = 1 quart
16 tablespoons = 1 cup
16 ounces net weight = 1 pound
2 cups = 1 pint
4 cups = 1 quart
4 quarts = 1 gallon

Send us your favorite recipe

and the memory that makes it special for you!*

....

If we select your recipe for a brand-new **Gooseberry Patch** cookbook,
your name will appear right along with it...and you'll receive a
FREE copy of the book!

Submit your recipe on our website at
www.gooseberrypatch.com/sharearecipe

*Please include the number of servings and all other necessary information.

Have a taste for more?

Visit www.gooseberrypatch.com to join our Circle of Friends!

....

- Free recipes, tips and ideas plus a complete cookbook index
- Get mouthwatering recipes and special email offers delivered to your inbox.

You'll also love these cookbooks from **Gooseberry Patch**!

150 Recipes in a 13x9 Pan

400-Calorie Slow-Cooker Recipes

5-Ingredient Family Favorite Recipes

America's Comfort Foods

Best Church Suppers

Comfort Food Lightened Up

Delicious Recipes for Diabetics

Fall Family Recipes

Foolproof Christmas

Meals in Minutes: 15, 20, 30

One-Pot Wonders

Rush Hour Recipes

Secrets from Grandma's Kitchen

Suppers in a Snap

www.gooseberrypatch.com